Three Steps
on the Ladder
of Writing

Previously Published Wellek Library Lectures

The Breaking of the Vessels
Harold Bloom

In the Tracks of Historical Materialism
Perry Anderson

Forms of Attention
Frank Kermode

Memoires for Paul de Man
Jacques Derrida

The Ethics of Reading
J. Hillis Miller

Peregrinations: Law, Form, Event
Jean-François Lyotard

Reopening of Closure: Organicism Against Itself
Murray Krieger

Musical Elaborations
Edward W. Said

Editorial Note

The Wellek Library Lectures in Critical Theory are given annually at the University of California, Irvine, under the auspices of the Critical Theory Institute. The following lectures were given in May 1990.

The Critical Theory Institute
Mark Poster, Director

I dedicate this book to Marguerite Sandré, who has been embodying for so many years the living and always present memory of my seminars.

Hélène Cixous

CONTENTS

Three Steps on the Ladder of Writing

The School of the Dead

Let us go to the school of writing, where we'll spend three school days initiating ourselves in the strange science of writing, which is a science of farewells. Of reunitings.

I will begin with: H

This is what writing is.

I speak to you today (today April 24, 1990, today June 24, 1990) through two languages. From one day to another, from one page to the other, writing changes languages. I have thought certain mysteries in the French language that I cannot think in English. This loss and this gain are in writing too. I have drawn the H. You will have recognized it depending on which language you are immersed in. This is what writing is: I

one language, I another language, and between the two, the line that makes them vibrate; writing forms a passageway between two shores.

H: you see the stylized outline of a ladder. This is the ladder writing climbs; the one that is important to me. Perhaps you were going to tell me this H is an *H*. I mean the letter *H*. After all, in French *H* is a letter rich in significance. Indeed, I write *H*, and I hear *hache* (axe). *H* is pronounced *ash* in French. This is already transporting for whosoever desires to write. In addition to this *hache*—a cutting instrument, an axe to clear new paths—the letter is granted uncommon favors in the French alphabet. If *A* is masculine, as is *B*, *C*, *D*, *E*, etc., only *H* is masculine, neuter, or feminine at will. How could I not be attached to *H*?

In addition, in French, *H* is a letter out of breath. Before it was reduced to silence during the French Empire, it was breathed out, aspirated. And it remembers this, even if we forget. It protects *le héros, la hardiesse, la harpe, l'harmonie, le hasard, la hauteur, l'heure* from any excessive hurt.

I can only tell you these mysteries silently in French. But in English there's breath; let's keep it.

I was saying: this H, this ladder is writing. This is how I figure it: the ladder is neither immobile nor empty. It is animated. It incorporates the movement it arouses and inscribes. My ladder is frequented. I say *my* because of my love for it: it's climbed by those authors I feel a mysterious affinity for; affinities, choices, are always secret.

The School of the Dead

When choosing a text I am called: I obey the call of certain texts or I am rejected by others. The texts that call me have different voices. But they all have one voice in common, they all have, with their differences, a certain music I am attuned to, and that's the secret. You may already know the ones whose music I hear. I have brought them with me, I will make them resound. There is *Clarice Lispector,* whose music is dry, hard, and severe, like *Bernhard's.* There is the more tender, melodious music of *Tsvetaeva,* or the more heartrending music of *Ingeborg Bachmann.* All these people frequented the same ladder. To us this ladder has a *descending* movement, because the ascent, which evokes effort and difficulty, is toward the bottom. I say *ascent* downward because we ordinarily believe the descent is easy. The writers I love are *descenders,* explorers of the lowest and deepest. Descending is deceptive. Carried out by those I love the descent is sometimes intolerable, the descenders descend with difficulty; sometimes they stop descending, like *Kafka:*

> "You say I should go down further still, but I am already very deep down, and yet, if it must be so, I will stay here. What a place! It is probably the deepest place there is. But I will stay here, only do not force me to climb down any deeper." [1]

(You may know that Kafka was two people and sometimes addresses himself as "thou," as did Leonardo da Vinci.)

There are two ways of clambering downward—by plunging into the earth and going deep into the sea—and neither is easy.

The element (and I would like to have you hear this word said by Tsvetaeva, in Russian: *stikhia,* she means both the element—matter—and the element—poetic verse—the word element signifies both things in Russian), *the element resists:* the earth and the sea offer resistance, as does language or thought. But when you descend into the earth, I imagine you mine the earth like a miner and go down feet first. Perhaps this is wrong, perhaps we must imagine a descent into the earth that is not feet first. And when you descend into the sea, then you can imagine whatever you wish: head first and you are in a fetal position—perhaps birth is toward the bottom or the other way up, or straight ahead standing upright. . . . The body inscribes part of its effort, depending on its position and need, in order to descend and work against the current, against the earth. It inscribes the orientation of its drives. Which is difficult. When we climb up toward the bottom, we proceed carried in the direction of—we're searching for something: the unknown. . . .

We will use this ladder, traveling along the steps, the moments, like periods, eras, airs (*ères* in French—*ères/airs*—look out for this phonetic play on words), epochs, leading toward the deepest. Toward what I call: *the truth,* toward what calls me, attracts me magnetically, irresistibly. Of course, I circle "the truth" with all kinds of signs, quotation marks, and brackets, to protect it from any form of fixation or conceptualization, since it is one of those words that constantly crosses our universe in a dazzling wake, but is also pursued by suspicion. I will talk about truth again, without which (without the word *truth,* without the mystery *truth*) there would be no writing. It is what writing *wants*. But it "(the truth)" is totally down below and a long way off. And all the people I love and whom I have mentioned are beings who are bent on directing their writing toward this *truth*-over-there, with unbelievable labor; they are fighting against the elements and principally against the innumerable immediate exterior and interior enemies. The exterior is very powerful at the present time. We are living particles, fireflies in the world, and around us resounds an enormous concert of noise-and-rumor-producing machines, creating a din and rumors destined to ensure we don't hear the voice of truth. But the interior enemies are just as numerous. It concerns our fear: this is what we are made of: our weakness. Kafka told us: paradise is not lost. We are the ones who haven't yet regained it, and if we haven't regained it, it's because we are suffering from two vices: laziness and impatience. As a result, we do nothing and don't advance, we stop out of laziness, hurry from impatience. Between the two, the work of descending isn't accomplished. Paradise is down below. According to my people, writing isn't given. Giving oneself to writing means being in a position to do this work of digging, of unburying, and this entails a long period of apprenticeship, since it obviously means going to school; writing is the right school. What I have learned cannot be generalized, but it can be shared. There are important moments of apprenticeship. The first moment of writing is the School of the Dead, and the second moment of writing is the School of Dreams. The third moment, the most advanced, the highest, the deepest, is the School of Roots.

◧

Today, on this first day, this first hour of the journey, we will go to the School of the Dead. I had announced that we would go to the *School of the Worst*. This was inaccurate: I dared not say in my letter that on the first day we would go to the dead.

◧

1. We Need a Dead(wo)man to Begin

To begin (writing, living) we must have death. I like the dead, they are the doorkeepers who while closing one side "give" way to the other.

We must have death, but young, present, ferocious, fresh death, the death of the day, today's death. The one that comes right up to us so suddenly we don't have time to avoid it, I mean to avoid feeling its breath touching us. Ha!

Because afterward most of us spend our lives *not seeing* the picture of Alexander's death hanging in the classroom:

> Death is in front of us, rather as on the schoolroom wall there is a reproduction of Alexander's Battle. The thing is to darken, or even indeed to blot out, the picture in this one life of ours through our actions.[2]

It's true that neither death nor the doorkeepers are enough to open the door. We must also have the courage, the desire, to approach, to go to the door.

Writing is this effort not to obliterate the picture, not to forget: this is how it is for Lispector, for Tsvetaeva, for Ingeborg Bachmann. . . . All those I have loved, each one for his or her different language, each one according to his or her voice, smile, tears, each one different from the others. Until I discovered later that in the beginning each one of them had an inaugural scene, from which writing sprouted.

Because it is always a question of a scene with a picture. The picture is the open door we must go through. Here is the birth scene of writing for *Thomas Bernhard:*

> This path took me past a butcher's shop. Open doors, axes, knives, cleavers, tidily arranged, slaughtering instruments some bloody, others shining and clean, slaughtering pistols, then the noise of the horses collapsing, those huge open bellies vomiting bones, pus, blood. Then past the butcher's, a few steps leading to the cemetery, to the morgue, to the tomb. During the first day, I still remember in addition a pale youth exhibited at the morgue, the son of a cheese-maker, and from there, my heart still beating on my schoolroom seat, a young womanschoolteacher. My grandmother always took me with her. Moreover, in the mornings I walked alone in front of the cemetery. In the afternoon, she took me to visit the morgue. She picked me up saying "Look, a woman lying there. Nothing but corpses." [3]

◧

I immediately recognized the way to school. As future skinned animals, to go to school we must pass before a butcher's shop, through the slaughter, to the cemetery door. Through the cemetery, our hearts beating from so much death, until we reach young life. This is our primary school, the school before school. The school to get to school. Where I went throughout my childhood, out of luck and necessity.

I lived in Clos Salembier, in the upper outskirts of Algiers, and to get to school everyday I passed (I went by bus, the K line) in front of the Catholic cemetery. The Catholic cemetery was my death as a Jewish girl. The cemetery spoke Latin. It said to me: *o mors, spes, et victoria*. I heard *le mors* (*the horse's bit*), *l'espèce* (*the species*); a horse resisted, who(se) was (the) victory? Everything happened to me in the cemetery, in a hostile manner.

It isn't by accident that we find in our memories the cemetery in front of the school once again. The first apprenticeship is the school with a cemetery. Kafka, who didn't go by a foreign—they are always foreign—cemetery, had the battle in front of his eyes in the classroom. We then spend our lives not seeing *what we saw*. The picture is there: what we know when we are small; when we are small, we know everything in a childlike way.

I said that the first dead are our first masters, those who unlock the door for us that opens onto the other side, if only we are willing to bear it. Writing, in its noblest function, is the attempt to unerase, to unearth, to find the primitive picture again, ours, the one that frightens us. Strangely, it concerns a scene. The picture is not there without a reason. Those who have been in contact with this opening door perceived it in the theatrical form of a scene. Why a scene? Why is it a scene? Why will it become the scene of the crime? Because we are the *audience* of this scene: we are not *in* the scene; when we go to the *theater* we are not on stage. We are witnesses to an extraordinary scene whose secret is on the other side. We are not the ones who have the secret. It's a pictorial scene.

The opening scene of "My Pushkin" by Tsvetaeva begins with a picture:

> It begins like a chapter in that novel, that indispensable bedside book of our mothers and grandmothers—*Jane Eyre*—the *mystery* of the red room.
>
> In the red room, a mysterious cabinet.
>
> But before the mysterious cabinet, there was something else: a picture in my mother's room—"The Duel." [4]

The duel represents the death of Pushkin. First there is the picture, which we either enter or don't enter. The duel—death—and the picture form a door, a window, an opening. Montaigne said philosophizing is learning to die. Writing is learning to die. It's learning not to be afraid, in other words to live at the extremity of life, which is what the dead, death, give us.

I'll say this in parenthesis: perhaps the dead man is the one who gives, while the dead woman gives less, I don't know. I'm showing my ignorance. Perhaps the dead man and not the dead woman enables us to receive; I'm talking about the father or mother, or whoever is in the place of the father or mother. Perhaps we can't receive from the dead mother what the dead father gives us? The dead man's death gives us the essential primitive experience, access to the other world, which is not without warning or noise but which is without the loss of our birthplace. So it gives us everything, it gives us the end of the world; to be human we need to experience the end of the world. We need to lose the world, to lose a world, and to discover that there is more than one world and that the world isn't what we think it is. Without that, we know nothing about the mortality and immortality we carry. We don't know we're alive as long as we haven't encountered death: these are banalities that have been erased. And it *is* an act of grace.

Dostoyevsky received the world through having lost it (we always come back to the experience of Abraham and Isaac), received it because he was condemned to death, because he was in front of a firing squad and then was pardoned, in extremis. This is grace: death given, then taken back.

Of course, I'm only talking about the death of the loved one, it's only a question of love here. And of everything loss brings as it takes away. We lose and in losing we win. This doesn't happen together, it can happen in a deferred, sustained, or continuous manner. As far as Bernhard is concerned, we might say that losing became winning in a fulgurating continuity. He tells the story of how he began writing: he was hospitalized at the age of eighteen and declared beyond all hope. His grandfather, whom he adored, was in the same hospital, and doing well, he tells us, then suddenly passed away. Bernhard: "I began to write hundreds and hundreds of poems." This is admirable, because it in-

William Morris

Willow
Lily
larkspur
chrysanthemum
artichoke
thistle
rose & roseleaf
iris
blackthorn
pimpernel
honeysuckle
wild rose
clover

my own designs

Churchyard

scribes an overabundance in its apparent realism, an extraordinarily vital stream. "I existed only when I was writing." We comprehend that it is necessary to write, to no longer stop, since not dying and writing have been exchanged. "And since my grandfather the poet was dead, now I had the right to write and I used the entire world, transforming it into poems." Here the cause of this spring of writing, which occurs as an answer, or an erection, as resistance to castration, is said brutally. But I prefer to talk about it in terms of feminine sexuality, as a vital spring brought about and ordered by the disappearance of the one who was the source. The grandfather wasn't just anyone, he was the poet, the one who had always loved him, who was everything to him.

In "Pertencer" Clarice Lispector has similarly told us how she had been conceived in the hope that her sick mother would survive, in the superstitious fantasy that if the mother produced life she would be cured.[5] Which didn't happen. The mother died. Clarice reveals in a dry voice how after her mother's death she always considered herself to be the soldier who deserted. And yet this happened without her being able to do anything about it. This is what we sometimes have difficulty hearing or accepting: we can do nothing about it. And yet desertion, flight, impotency, are printed on the classroom wall. They are linked, associated: there is death. The misfortune or fortune—which will make our lives an unending struggle to be fair—is that *in losing we have something to gain*. Mixed loss and gain: that's our crime. This is what we are always guilty of, guilt we can't do anything about with these unexpected and terrible gains.

The first book I wrote rose from my father's tomb. I don't know why, perhaps it was the only thing I had to write then, in my poverty, my inexperience, the *only asset:* the only thing that made me live, that I had lived, that put me to the test, and that I felt because it completely defeated me. It was my strange and monstrous treasure. I didn't think about all this, otherwise I wouldn't have written. For a long time I lived through my father's death with the feeling of immense loss and childlike regret, as in an inverted fairy tale: Ah if my father had lived! I naively fabricated other magnificent stories, until the day things changed color and I began to see other scenes—including everything I could imagine that was less consoling—without overinvesting. I had moved on to less idealized reflection, to reconstruction. I could imagine various scenes without my father: the perfect scene (but which one?), the imperfect scene, the scene of interdiction, the commonplace one, the classic one: don't write. And I said to myself that I wouldn't have written. . . . I wouldn't have had death, if my father had lived. I have written this several times: he gave me death. To start with.

Recently my mother, who is a simple and straightforward soul, read one of my books and said to me: so your father's death was that serious for you. Yes, I said, and I've told you this a hundred times. But doubtless the message didn't get through, and I calmly explained what I am telling you. To which my mother replied: For me too. I know that my mother lost my father all her life, she has been without her husband, her young husband, and that this was a real loss, she lost the man she loved. And she said: By chance, he is dead. If not she would never have become who she is. When my father was alive, my mother didn't work, because my father had a young, primitive Jew's dignity—he was the one who should provide for the family. My mother became a midwife after my father's death. She conducted hundreds and hundreds of deliveries, having vaguely elaborated what cannot be said in words. What is liberated by a straightforward and simple soul's mourning can also be life.

We don't know, either universally or individually, exactly what our relationship to the dead is. Individually, it constitutes part of our work, our work of love, not of hate or destruction; we must think through each relationship. We can think this with the help of writing, if we know how to write, if we dare write. Also with the help of dreams: they give us the marvelous gift of constantly bringing back our dead alive, with the result that at night we can talk with our dead. Each of us, individually and freely, must do the work that consists of rethinking what is your death and my death, which are inseparable. Writing originates in this relationship. In what is often inadmissible, contrary, terribly dangerous, and risks turning into complacency—which is the worst of all crimes: it originates here. We are the ones who make of death something mortal and negative. Yes, it is mortal, it is bad, but it is also good; this depends on us. We can be the killers of the dead, that's the worst of all, because when we kill a dead person, we kill ourselves. But we can also, on the contrary, be the guardian, the friend, the regenerator of the dead.

Writing is this complex activity, "this learning to die," that is, not to kill, knowing there is death, not denying it and not proclaiming it. . . . Our crime isn't what we think, it isn't the crime in the newspapers, it's always a bit less and a bit more. In life, as soon as I say *my,* as soon as I say *my* daughter, *my* brother, I am verging on a form of murder, as soon as I forget to unceasingly recognize the other's difference. You may come to know your son, your sister, your daughter well after thirty, forty, or fifty years of life, and yet during those thirty or forty years you haven't known this person who was so close. You kept him or her in the realm of the dead. And the other way around. Then the one who dies kills and the one who doesn't die when the other dies kills as well.

Surviving is not what we think: this is what Lydia Tchoukovskaia confides to us in *La Plongée.*[6] This woman, who was Anna Akhmatova and Nadejda Mandelstam's friend, belonged to the small universe of women struck by the same misfortune, women from whom half the body, half the soul, the child, the lover, the spouse had been torn. For the Soviets, in their bizarre madness during the years of darkness, sent millions of Russians to concentration camps, but, inexplicably, often let the wives "survive." Anna Akhmatova, who lost a first husband, executed by firing squad, a second husband, deported then executed, and whose son was deported, had Nadejda Mandelstam for a friend, whose husband, the great poet, was deported for poetry. And then Lydia Tchoukovskaia's husband was deported because he was a Jewish scholar. When he was arrested Lydia was notified of the verdict: "Ten years without the right to correspond." So, like hundreds of women, she lined up with parcels in front of the prison walls—until the day she learned that "ten years without the right to correspond" was a metaphor for: immediate execution. For several years she had been carrying inside herself a living deadman, alive within her, decomposing outside her.

This is the story of Edgar Allan Poe's "Mr. Valdemar."[7] Mr. Valdemar calls the narrator, who is a hypnotist, telling him to come quickly since he is about to die. It is time, according to their pact, for him to hypnotize the dying man. The narrator arrives. Mr. Valdemar doesn't hear the narrator, who has just enough time to catch his breath and put him to sleep. After rather a long time, we feel that Mr. Valdemar, who is now in a hypnotic state, is suffering terribly. When the narrator "wakes up" Mr. Valdemar, the sleeper's life breaks out in a flow of pus because he "was" dead. This is Tchoukovskaia's story, the loved one remained inside her, a dead man inexplicably without his death.

Tchoukovskaia tells us about "plunging" as if it's drinking or eating. She says: "I am going to plunge." This plunge is her way of going to write. The book begins with something dreadful: she screams at night and it's always the same dream, she dreams that her dead husband has come back; he walks past her, he looks at her with hatred, acts as if he doesn't know her, and goes to speak to other people. Each time it's the same cruel dream which she doesn't understand. Hatred burns between them. Until suddenly one day she understands the hatred this man she loves so much has shown her. She understands *her* hatred. *Her own hatred. Their hatred:* which satisfies itself in her dreams. She is staging an unenvisionable crime. What she lives out, and what she rejects with all her strength, is the fact that the deadman reproaches her for being alive. This is something she cannot come to terms with since she is both characters at once, herself and her-him. She is guilty of being a survivor. She didn't follow him. She isn't him.

We know these returns. I've lived many of them. In *If This Is a Man* Primo Levi speaks of the dream he has, which is, he says, a dream all the deportees had, the absolute nightmare, the dream of the impossible return.[8] The deportee returns to his family, everyone is at the table, and he is not received, they don't listen to him, they don't believe him, they don't understand him. They deprive him of his suffering. They take away his dreadful possession, his truth as a tortured prisoner. He is guilty of being a victim. It is experience turned inside out.

Not dying, living after the other, "remaining," is also an intolerable experience. It is at this point that we feel, though we can do nothing about it, that there may be the *unpardonable in ourselves*. There is a murder that assassinates us, it's not you, it's not me, but between you and me, between my love and your love there is murder. All great texts are prey to the question: who is killing me? Whom am I giving myself to kill? We passionately love murder stories: we believe we are reading one of Dostoyevsky's books, but what we are tasting is the account of our own murders.

The Notebooks for the Idiot are haunted by this initial nucleus from which *The Idiot* was born. *The Idiot* is the book that survived many other books. The book that will be published is the strongest, the one that mysteriously survived all the others. Beneath this book there are hundreds of books that weren't written, that were gradually pushed aside. In *The Notebooks for the Idiot* hundreds of books that were proposed, erased, and, at the same time, reproduced so that *The Idiot* could exist, lie helplessly in ruins. The initial story, the starting shot from which *The Idiot* arose was—anecdotally or unanecdotally—a news item: a young sixteen-year-old girl, Umetskaïa, had killed her entire family after having been victimized. She is there throughout *The Notebooks*, she is constantly transformed, sometimes she's a man, sometimes a woman, sometimes young, sometimes old. She will end up dividing herself between Nastasia Philipovna and Rogojine. Dostoyevsky was prey to this character's mystery: what causes a young woman to bloody the entire house. She is a monster who isn't a monster. I could be her. I who am also you.

> From his upbringing and his surroundings he early imbibed this poison, which had penetrated his very bloodstream. [The Idiot himself is the criminal at that moment.] His magnanimity and his

yearning for love derive in general from an infinitely outraged heart. He has never <been able to heal those wounds>, and therefore he has retaliated and revenged himself on all those he would have liked to love without limit and to shed his very blood for all those *dear* to him.

Instead of useful activity—evil. . . .

Or else he sat down one day and wrote out his will. He wanted to kill himself, but didn't, instead he began an intrigue.

They set fire to the house.

A precious question and answer:

"You will end up either by committing a great crime, or by performing a great deed"—says the son to him.

"God willing!" he replied quite seriously, and faintly, "But more likely by nothing of the sort."

(He is yearning to do some noble deed, so as to distinguish himself and surpass everyone else. They set the house on fire, and the burned finger.) . . .

N.B. He loves Umetskaia. A strange and *utterly* childlike friendship with the *yurodivaia*. . . .

She never instructs him as to his duties toward his wife, she merely acts.

In the country she had *twice* set fire to a barn, so as to be like Olga Umetskaia.

She set a fire in Petersburg, too.

Perhaps it would be far better to make him a legitimate son.

"Set up a detailed plan and tonight *begin*." . . .

Then die well; one can die well even when spitting one's last, vanity, the baby, your sufferings, mountains—

When it becomes necessary—why not speak out?—Since you wanted to shoot yourself, why, shoot yourself. . . .

To the hospital, spittle, how stupid I am. . . .

"You make too much of a furor about your dying. One can die more nobly."

> "Well, shoot yourself. As if you frighten us."
>
> "But I don't allow you to, no, I don't allow it."
>
> "Talk to me a little about Christ, Prince."
>
> "Since I have only 2 weeks more, telling *the truth* or lying is absolutely the same to me." . . .
>
> Why is it necessary in the construction of the world that there should be people condemned to die?[9]

Would you like to know why? Read *The Notebooks of the Idiot* and you'll know everything: we need those who are condemned to death and we need books that "condemn" us.

Here is what Kafka wrote in 1904 to his friend Pollak:

> I think we ought to only read the kind of books that wound and stab us. If the book we are reading doesn't wake us up with a blow on the head, what are we reading it for? So that it will make us happy, as you write? Good Lord, we would be happy precisely if we had no books, and the kind of books that make us happy are the kind we could write ourselves if we had to. But we need the books that affect us like a disaster, that grieve us deeply, like the death of someone we loved more than ourselves, like being banished into forests far from everyone, like a suicide. A book must be the axe for the frozen sea inside us. That is my belief.[10]

He wrote this letter because his friend had reproached him for not having answered his letters. Kafka answers him by saying: excuse me, but I was reading. The book was so important I couldn't stop. Always the same violent relationship: the book first, then you.

I too believe we should only read those books that "wound" us and "stab" us, "wake us up with a blow on the head" or strike us like terrible events, that do and don't do us good, that don't do us good in doing us good, a book "like the death of someone we loved more than ourselves," or that is "like being banished into forests far from everyone," or books that are "like a suicide." Or as he says at the end: a book "must be the axe for the frozen sea inside us."

That is what I believe but it also saddens me because very few books are axes, very few books hurt us, very few books break the frozen sea. Those books that do break the frozen sea and kill us are the books that give us joy. Why are such books so rare? Because those who write the books that hurt us also suffer, also undergo a sort of suicide, also get lost in forests—and this is frightening. You do not want to lose your life so easily in writing, yet this is what Clarice Lispector did. Not only did she do this metaphorically, she also did this in reality. Not only do her books try to be the axe, but, at the end of her rather short life, she wrote *The Hour of the Star,* which actually deals with the life and death of a character called Macabea, a kind of woman, a person who is so slight she almost does not exist.[11] Thoughout the writing of the book everyone is terrified, the writer is terrified, the book is terrified; the text starts telling us something, then it gives up. We feel as if something terrible is going to happen and we readers are also frightened: we keep thinking that something we don't want to happen will happen, only it doesn't happen. We go with misgivings from page to page. And suddenly it happens: the text strikes, the book is finished, Macabea is dead. But not only is Macabea dead, Clarice Lispector is also dead, she died immediately afterward. The book has achieved in the most truthful way possible the reality, the secret of writing. Clarice Lispector was ill. She did not know she was going to die, but she knew it the moment she finished this book. One does not really know who wrote the book or who killed who. One does not know whether Clarice Lispector wrote the book in haste because she thought she was going to die or whether the book put an end to her life. Because of this strange connection between writing and dying writers feel a strange desire for death. They feel like dying. But it is something they cannot say. I can't say: "I feel like dying," because it is forbidden, and yet it is really the only thing one should say.

The writers I feel close to are those who play with fire, those who play seriously with their own mortality, go further, go too far, sometimes go as far as catching fire, as far as being seized by fire. How terrible to learn how Ingeborg Bachmann perished—burned by fire, that is, by truth—in 1971 in Rome, while in the same period Clarice Lispector was pulled from the flames by her son: how terrible and how amazing!

I find the same desires, the same cries in the introduction to Ingeborg Bachmann's *Franza:*

> I have often wondered, and you too I suppose, what has become of the virus of crime? It cannot suddenly have disappeared from the universe.[12]

She wrote this introduction at a time in Austria when anti-Semitism, Holocaust, and desecration were underground. "Of course, massacres belong to the past," she writes, adding: "the assassins are still among us." She wrote that at a time when we might have thought we had buried Auschwitz. What she writes is dangerous because Auschwitz is always there in every human being.

In an interview in which she talks about her books she says everything is war. War doesn't begin with the first bombs that are dropped, it doesn't begin with the terror recounted in the newspapers: it begins in the relationships between people. She also insists: "Facism is the first thing in the relationship between a man and a woman, I have tried to say that here, that in this society it's always war. Not that there is war and peace, there is only war."[13] It's harsh, but that's her, in truth, in the Austrian predicament.

In France we also say that there is war, but we also say we are subjects of peace. But for Austria there is only war.

2. That the Act of Reading or Writing Be a Mortal Act; or, Reading/Writing, Escape in Broad Daylight

Not everyone carries out the act of reading in the same way, but there is a manner of reading comparable to the act of writing—it's an act that suppresses the world. We annihilate the world with a book. You take the book you have opened, either knowingly or unknowingly, but often with an intimation that this book may be an instrument of separation. As soon as you open the book as a door, you enter another world, you close the door on this world. Reading is escaping in broad daylight, it's the rejection of the other; most of the time it's a solitary act, exactly like writing. We don't always think of this because we no longer read; we used to read when we were children and knew how violent reading can be. The book strikes a blow, but you, with your book, strike the outside world with an equal blow. We cannot write in any other way—without slamming the door, without cutting the ties.

The writer is a secret criminal. How? First because writing tries to undertake that journey toward strange sources of art that are foreign to us. "The thing" does not happen here, it happens somewhere else, in a strange and foreign country. The writer has a foreign origin; we do not know about the particular nature of these foreigners, but we feel they feel there is an appeal, that someone is calling them back.

The author writes as if he or she were in a foreign country, as if he or she were a foreigner in his or her own family. We don't know the authors, we read books and we take them for the authors. We think there must be an analogy or identification between the book and the author. But you can be sure there is an immense difference between the author and the person who wrote; and if you were to meet that person, it would be someone else. The foreign origin of the book makes the scene of writing a scene of immeasurable separation. Is Rembrandt "Dutch"? He always painted "in foreign countries." His paintings, which paint painting, are inhabited by extraordinary people, foreigners. Everyone has been struck by the fact that Rembrandt constantly painted Jews, imaginary Jews, bedecked Jews: calm, doubly foreign as Jews and as bedizened beings, triply hyperoriental and foreign in their looks. It is as if this strange man had passed through the painting's shadow toward the far distant source, the foreign source from which he painted, he who was more than a man of his country, more than the issue of Dutch soil.

Look for instance at Rembrandt's picture entitled "The Jewish Fiancée." It is softly strange. It is also a metaphor for Rembrandt's entire work, which is full of familiar foreigners, full of Jews and oriental people who do not belong to Rembrandt's family. Yet they belong to this other world or he to theirs. As if he were painting to discover his secret foreign origin. We write, we paint, throughout our entire lives as if we were going to a foreign country, as if we were foreigners inside our own families, "hinaus in die Fremde der Heimat," as Celan writes, that is where we go.[14] Between the writer and his or her family the question is always one of departing while remaining present, of being absent while in full presence, of escaping, of abandon. It is both utterly banal and the thing we don't want to know or say. A writer has no children; I have no children when I write. When I write I escape myself, I uproot myself, I am a virgin; I leave from within my own house and I don't return. The moment I pick up my pen—magical gesture—I forget all the people I love; an hour later they are not born and I have never known them. Yet we do return. But for the duration of the journey we are killers. (Not only when we write, when we read too. Writing and reading are not separate, reading is a part of writing. A real reader is a writer. A real reader is already on the way to writing.)

◧

3. What is Reading? It's Eating on the Sly

It's also a clandestine, furtive act. We don't acknowledge it. It confuses. Reading is not as insignificant as we claim. First we must steal the key to the library. Reading is a provocation, a rebellion: we open the book's door, pretending it is a simple paperback cover, and in broad daylight escape! We are no longer there: this is what real reading is. If we haven't left the room, if we haven't gone over the wall, we're not reading. If we're only making believe we're there, if we're pretending before the eyes of the family, then we're reading. We are eating. Reading is eating on the sly.

Reading is eating the forbidden fruit, making forbidden love, changing eras, changing families, changing destinies, and changing day for night. Reading is doing everything exactly as we want and "on the sly."

And what books do we read as we become strangers in joy? Those that teach us how to die.

For example Montaigne, our textual grandfather.

"Montaigne." This is the title of a short text by Thomas Bernhard that I read with delight as "The Tale of Writing." A crafty tale, written in a single flight, at the pace of a single race, miming the scene of concealed reading.

The title announces: "Montaigne." I might think, like you, that this text will deal with Montaigne the author. Will it be a portrait? "Montaigne" in the nude, plain "Montaigne," announces nothing beyond Montaigne. "Montaigne" puts us in a state of Montaigne.

So we think this will be a portrait of Montaigne or that it will return to Montaigne, the head of the text.

And this is where the text starts, by fleeing. In flight. Written to flee a death threat. The flight and the fugitive's panting will trace the text's path and rhythm. Taking off from "Montaigne," the narration and narrator race in Montaigne's direction:

> *In order to flee my family and therefore my executioners,* I took refuge in a corner of the tower, and without light and hence without maddening the mosquitoes against me, I had taken from the library a book which after I had read a few sentences turned out to be by Montaigne with whom I am, *in a certain intimate and actually enlightening way, a relative more than with anybody else.*[15]

Montaigne whom he loves best. And the whole of this short adventure deals with that choice in darkness.

This is how it starts and it then goes on to tell the adventure of reading that book. The text is a real lesson in writing, paragraph by paragraph, step by step, as if you were inside the tower and climbing step by step—I won't tell you if it is up or down—in complete obscurity.

The text flees paragraph by paragraph. "Montaigne" comes to an end in twenty-two steps or paragraphs—twenty-two bounds. Since you read with your body, your body paragraphs. The steps are almost comparable in size. Sometimes a bit shorter or a bit longer. And they are all equally dense and urgent.

It is immediately about the essential experiences of our lives. No sooner do we enter than we take flight. In the first paragraph we already have a series of directions. And each one of them will be pursued, none of them will be abandoned by the text. However, for the major part of this text, we run and flee in the dark: "I took refuge in a corner of the tower, and without light. . . . I had taken . . . a book. . . . In absolute darkness I had taken a book from the library." A blind choice, I choose precisely Montaigne, with whom "I am . . . a relative more than with anybody else." I choose from amongst them all—and without having chosen him, hence *blindly*—my relative.

> Montaigne with whom I am, in a certain intimate and actually enlightening way, a relative more than with anybody else.

Here's the light, in the relationship with Montaigne. It is an enlightening relationship.

Third paragraph:

> On the way which led me to the tower, where as I have said I did not put on the light because of the mosquitoes, I tried very consciously, with the greatest concentration, to guess which book I had picked up on the shelf, but all the philosophers who went through my head, were all possible philosophers except Montaigne.[16]

The light comes from inside, the book comes through the head (mine). Montaigne comes to him from within, like necessity itself.

This is already a lesson in true reading; reading we cannot dissociate from our lives. Reading, which establishes another universe of light and dark to that of the outside world, and which is obviously the prolongation of the universe of writing. This happens in intimacy, where sunlight does not reign, reigned over by another light.

That is what we do, we pick up something in the dark. We don't know what we will pick up. We always do this: we pick up a book, but we don't know why. And it happens to be our parent, since the only way to find our real parent is to pick up a book in the dark. It is mysterious. Maybe it is the parent on the shelf that has chosen us, but it can't be explained. Anyway, this is the way we happen on those books that will change our lives. Of course we have at least heard a signifier, but we do choose in this completely blind way and it turns out to be light. This is how Montaigne comes to Bernhard: as the totally unexpected and completely hoped for. All the philosophers go through his head except Montaigne. A subtle scene of overinvestment. The desire for Montaigne is so strong that he doesn't expect Montaigne. And Montaigne comes on the condition of being unexpected. He is absolutely unexpected. There must be an absence of light, plus light in the sentence in order to find Montaigne. Because, of course, light comes from inside and you cannot account for the arrival of light in your life and your head through books. Bernhard insists on this:

> So I read *my* Montaigne with the shutters locked in the most absurd way because it was extremely painful to read without artificial light.[17]

It was unimaginable—so he read Montaigne in complete darkness.

Eventually, we reach the point where Bernhard has read Montaigne and has come to this sentence:

> *Let us hope that nothing happened to him.* [N.B., Hélène Cixous's underlining.] This sentence was not from Montaigne, but from my family, which was looking for me and roaming round the foot of the tower in search of me.[18]

"Let us hope that nothing happened to him." We can taste all the sugar and salt and bitterness of this sentence once we have read everything that precedes it. On a realistic level the parents appear to be worried (I'm talking about the contents of the sentence, not about the intervention of the sentence in the text). If we have a sense of irony we hear: we hope he hasn't read anything, that nothing has happened in that terrible tower, in particular that Montaigne hasn't arrived, etc. . . . We could unravel the sentence forever. One world is being swallowed by another. I was reading Montaigne until the sentence came. The continuity is wonderful. Bernhard doesn't say whether this sentence is inside or outside. The sentence bumps into him. It is imagined as if it were a dream. Are you in your dream or are you already outside? The sentence that has just been uttered: is it still in the dream or is it already outside? Is it in the book or is it in you? It is delocalized. There is hesitation as to the sentence's origin because, after all, Montaigne isn't Montaigne: he is "my family." Montaigne and "my family" pass through the same parental place.

Now we don't know whether this sentence, which is the last sentence of the book, is heard inside or outside the tower. Just as we don't know whether the book happens inside or outside.

Why did Bernhard need to take refuge in the dark tower—Montaigne's tower, obviously—unless it was to save his life, which had been threatened since his earliest childhood by his executioner-family. Things are clear in the dark library. It concerns the deadly war waged between children and parents, this war that turns in circles and began before us all: fear and destruction weave their web between children and parents; you want to kill me, says one, no, you're the one who wants my death, says the other. And it's true, each one kills the other, on either side of the book: the object of passion. It's true: those who love texts incite the hatred of those who don't. It's true: one can kill for a book, for a poem. For or against. One can kill a poet on account of poetry. It's true: poetry—what poison to those who can't take it. For between us, readers and antireaders, there are crimes prompted by jouissance.

Our murders are decided in an obscure and violent relation to jouissance, in jealousy so dark, primitive, and remote we don't even see it. There, in the shadows, a scandalous scene of deprivation is played out: the parent would like to starve the child or at least use hunger to keep hold of him or her. And all this is not without love, not without hate.

If in the past I was frightened to death to take a lump of sugar from the sugarbowl in the dining room, today I am frightened to death to take a book from the library and I am even more frightened to death if it is a philosophy book, like last night.

In the beginning they told you: you must not drink this water, because it is poisoned. If you drink this water, you are heading for disaster, if you read this book, you are heading for disaster. They lead you into the forest, they put you in dark children's rooms, to disturb you, they introduce you to people you immediately recognize as those who will destroy you.[19]

We recognize the old grandiose and threatening hymn: you will not drink, you will not eat, you will not read, you will not write, otherwise, you will die.

And they call reading a sin, and writing is a crime.

And no doubt this is not entirely false.

They will never forgive us for this Somewhere Else.

Let's come back to the first words of this text; all this is done only "in order to escape." The text has been written in order to escape, to escape the family, etc.

Here is the last paragraph:

I read my Montaigne with the shutters locked in the most absurd way because it was extremely painful to read without artificial light. . . . Let us hope that nothing happened to him. This sentence was not from Montaigne, but from my family who were looking for me and were roaming round the foot of the tower in search of me.

We are still in the dark. Without artificial light: but not without light. We must be as refined as he is, everything is, so to speak, clear.

I come back to the beginning of the text. The text takes off at full speed, in order to escape. The escape is not carried out. All the while the others are there down below.

There is a relationship between reading and what engenders the need, the urgency of reading: you can't have one without the other. To escape

. . . I read. That's the mystery of reading. And no realism. One must stay on the side of the text. Accepting the fact that reading is carried out "with the shutters locked." It's both true and not true. We must constantly have one foot in one world and one in the other. This does not belong to the fantastic: it is misleading in Kafka's manner. You believe you are on a path, but you're on another, you're on that one, etc. Such is the relation between reading and writing. In the same way this text is written by the light of an inner Montaigne, in the dark. We write in the dark, we read in the dark: they are the same process.

4. The Author's Crime Has Its Legend

We owe this to the specialist of irrepressible crime—crime in writing—the demon of perversity: Edgar Allan Poe.

What do we do with the other when we create? What does the author do? What does the painter do? That is, what do we do? This is our portrait, the portrait of the artist done by himself or herself, the portrait of you by me: it is oval: the Egg of Evil. What do we do with the body of the other when we are in a state of creation—and with our own bodies too. We annihilate (ourselves) (Thomas Bernhard would say), we pine (ourselves) away (Edgar Allan Poe would say), we erase (ourselves) (Henry James would say). In short, we institute immurement. It all begins with walls. Those of the tower. Those of the château we enter as we follow a seriously wounded narrator.

"The Oval Portrait" starts like this:

> The château into which my valet had ventured to make forcible entrance [this is not "Montaigne," it is "The Oval Portrait"], rather than permit me, in my desperately wounded condition, to pass a night in the open air, was one of those piles of commingled gloom and grandeur which have so long frowned among the Apennines, not less in fact than in the fancy of Mrs. Radcliffe.[20]

As it starts, you as reader enter the wounded narrator's château. The narrator arrives in a strange room full of pictures, and his attention is caught by a particular oval portrait, which is so extraordinary that he does not believe his eyes. Little by little the story unravels in such a way that you become fixed, focused on the oval portrait: and the oval portrait has its own story that the narrator will read. You pass into the other story, which is the story within the story. This story, of the young woman's life and death, serves as model for the story. While you get into the story of the oval portrait you completely forget about the narrator; not only do you forget, but he completely disappears from the scene, and when the tale ends it ends inside the oval portrait—behind the wall of the portrait—and you as reader have committed something very strange: you have erased the narrator from your memory, you are in another scene. This is Poe's genius. When we read "The Oval Portrait," we think we are reading the story of "The Oval Portrait": the story of a painter who was a genius, who married a beauty who was life itself and started to paint her. This is what Poe says, or the narrator. I don't know who says it finally, because there is Poe, the narrator, and the writer of the book in which the oval portrait is described . . . so somebody says:

> "But he, the painter, took glory in his work, which went on from hour to hour, and from day to day. And he was a passionate, and wild, and moody man, who became lost in reveries; so that he would not see that the light which fell so ghastly in that lone turret withered the health and the spirits of his bride, who pined visibly to all but him. Yet she smiled on and still on . . . [—until at length all the life of the bride goes into the portrait—] at length, as the labour drew nearer to its conclusion, there were admitted none into the turret; for the painter had grown wild with the ardour of his work, and turned his eyes from the canvas rarely, even to regard the countenance of his wife. And he would not see that the tints which he spread upon the canvas were drawn from the cheeks of her who sat beside him. And when many weeks had passed, and but little remained to do, save one brush upon the mouth and one tint upon the eye, the spirit of the lady again flickered up as the flame within the socket of the lamp. And then the brush was given, and then the tint was placed; and, for one moment, the painter stood entranced

> before the work he had wrought; but in the next, while he yet gazed, he grew tremulous and very pallid, and aghast, and crying with a loud voice, 'This is indeed Life itself!' turned suddenly to regard his beloved:—She was dead![21]

And that is the end.

It is a kind of allegory for what happens in creation. It is mythical, it might also be considered a cliché. It is not, because in the course of reading we have ourselves become the painter. We too have followed and started painting and forgetting and erasing the narrator in particular, which is very strange. And I suspect we might even come out of the turret or the tale without ever realizing what we have done. This is the writer's crime. It is described by Poe. It is paroxystic and something he does often, almost as if he had feminist leanings, since he nearly always gives men the part of the killer and women the part of the victim.

I know a type of painter who did exactly the same thing. He painted his poems with the blush of the women he loved. I am talking about Rilke. He kept a diary called *Das Testament* during the last years of his life, when he was deeply in love with Merline.[22] It is composed of short fragments and was not supposed to be published during his lifetime. It was published fifty years later. It tells us uniquely of his relation to Merline/Mrs. Klossovska and to poetry. It is almost unbearable. It reveals a pining for poetry that is heartrending and at the same time involves a terrible war waged against this woman—though this is not expressed directly to her since she did not read the diary. There is also a large volume of letters exchanged between Rilke and his beloved, all of which say the same thing: don't come, don't approach me, don't kill me; that's what he says to her, because he must write. Sometimes he only saw her once in six months, and she, a powerful woman, did not enjoy the situation. She suffered and he suffered; and he explains everything about sublimation in beautiful letters.

N.B. I don't know whether this testament should have been published or not. It is true that you may be allowed to "murder" symbolically in intimacy, but if it comes out, if the crime has witnesses, it is terrible:

of course Rilke never thinks that he is murdering someone. He asks the woman he loves to accompany him in the sphere of poetry. At the same time he needs her to be real. Bernhard, on the contrary, will claim the crime directly. It is part of his power to say *directly:* "Will you excuse me, for I must kill you." Which renders his books extraordinarily cruel and, at the same time, bordering on the comic.

Let's go back inside the walls of "The Oval Portrait." I had been following the narrator for several pages. (So he is not a ghost narrator, for he takes up two thirds of the text.) The economy of our relation to the subject and the narration is an effect of the text but it's also linked to what the text is telling us. The narrator makes such a disappearing disappearance that we disinvest. We reinvest in the painter's scene: so that's it, farewell narrator! Yet we should worry about him, for he is seriously wounded. All this is the extraordinary staging of our capacity for repression. We the murderer-painter. This is the art of Edgar Allan Poe: he makes *us* carry out what is done in the text (here, by the painter).

The portrait is in the portrait, the book is in the book, and the last circle of this process tells us: be careful, if someone paints what happens to the model? What relation does the painter have to the model? (A banal yet indispensable question.) All painters' models ask it. Pirandello wrote the same story. It's the story of the person who gives life; it's the model who gives life whereas we think it's the painter. The painter is the one who takes the model's life. A metaphor for all the arts.

Bernhard says that at certain moments you have to cross over corpses, you have to kill someone in order to write. It's true and it's not true. Certain artists say it's true, others say it isn't. With Edgar Allan Poe there is an additional victim who is the narrator himself. With Poe we execute the narrator.

There is a secondary character in the narrative: *the audience. Us.* We are the onlookers in the brief story read in the book. The audience: a nonindividualized yet interested audience. It appears as the witness to a great love affair. The audience is clearly distinguished from the author, the "analyst" of this short volume. The audience says: you must love passionately in order to paint the young woman so well. The analyst tells us that the painter's relationship to his wife is a misfortune whereas the audience tells us it's good fortune. It is a reading position.

And then the audience is sent away; it isn't there when the crime takes place. There is no one to relate it except the anonymous narrator-analyst. We, as spectators of creation, are blind. We are lost in admiration for this great painter and do not know the price such a great work will cost. "I," the unknown narrator, knows it. The young woman knows it.

If we tried to derive from this short narrative a kind of ethic for the relation between the artist and the model, how might we read the last lines of the tale? In the nineteenth century the ethical relation between the creator and the created was an essential question. It also appears in Bernhard's texts. It's a recurrent theme in Poe. The antagonistic and deadly man-woman relationship is everywhere. There is not even any ambivalence: man is bad, woman is good. Many texts take up this simple opposition, others are more ambiguous: in these, on the contrary, sometimes the woman is good or bad, while the man is often in the painter's position.

Let's take the end of the text: as the painter looks at the painting, *he sees* for the first time. He has never seen before. Our narrator begins by seeing, then he works on this seeing: what did I see? I saw, etc. But the painter never saw. He is blind. It's only at the end, when "the thing" is finished (and it ends with "one tint" on the eye) that he takes a moment to regard. And in that moment he sees for the first time, he sees the truth. He sees: it is life itself that has been painted.

In the second moment: what he sees fills him with terror. Which means a redoubling of his blindness. He never wanted to do that. He cries: It's life, as if he were crying: It's death. In absolute terror.

In the third moment: he "turned suddenly," and as he turns, it's exactly what he feared seeing: she is dead. It is an analytical scene. God is not there. Although there is interdiction and permission. There will have been the superego but not God. What we are made to understand is that there can't be life on both sides. As the analyst tells us, the painter magically drew life, real, substantial, material life, from his wife's cheeks. We might expect him to be proud of the work but he can't be. We are made to understand: we cannot create in a just manner. In creation we find ourselves before the inevitable failure. It's a double bind: either you don't render life or you take it. Everything is a failure, *everything is crime.*

We, the spectators, would like to console ourselves and repress the scene's cruelty, saying that the end justifies the means. But we live in a feminist era and we protest: women are the ones who pay for the affair. We lose either art or life. The rest is truth.

What comes back to us, no matter what our place, is a duty to truth, to know what is at stake and not deny it.

This is the narrator's task in "The Oval Portrait." He saw at first glance; at the same time it's unbearable, and he needs a great deal of time to interiorize what he saw, to accept the terrible fulgurating facts. But, as the text implies, the narrator "is gifted for that," he accepts the sight of death because, from the beginning, he is mortally wounded. It is indeed necessary to have been wounded to tolerate seeing death ineluctably inscribed in the scene.

5. The Author Is in the Dark; or, The Self-Portrait of a Blind Painter

Like the painter in "The Oval Portrait" or like Rilke in *Das Testament* the author proceeds in a constituent blindness, which produces effects that can be good or bad. The fact that the author can perceive his or her darkness doesn't change the quality of the darkness.

It can also happen that an author will kill himself or herself writing. The only book that is worth writing is the one we don't have the courage or strength to write. The book that hurts us (we who are writing), that makes us tremble, redden, bleed. It is combat against ourselves, the author; one of us must be vanquished or die.

I don't want to write the true book; it's the one I want to write: I tear it from myself.

Thinking about these desired yet feared books is unsettling. I am afraid of the fire that devoured Clarice and Ingeborg, though at the same time I admire it. On the subject of *The Hour of the Star* I have written a great deal about just how far Clarice Lispector went in order to write the book that was forbidden her. I revolved around this violently magic little text.

It is the most extraordinary example of total exchange and merging with the soft and mysterious violence of writing. *The Hour of the Star* is the final book, and in order to write the final book Clarice Lispector had to transform herself, abandon herself, lose herself in a masculine author to the point of no return.

What torments me is that the person who writes and who is sensitive to this kind of danger cannot not have *the desire to die*. The desire to die is the one thing in the world we cannot permit ourselves to admit; I am not talking about suicide: the desire to die and the temptation of suicide are two different things; suicide is murder, suicide is aimed at someone or something, whereas the desire to die is not this at all—which is why we can't talk about it. Some people have spoken about this poetically and directly. Clarice Lispector spoke about this through Macabea but without emphasizing that she was thereby expressing her desire to die. While she was weaving Macabea's death, she wrote in her notebooks:

> The only way to know if life exists after death is to believe while still being alive. I wanted to die once and come back to life—simply in order to know the juice of life that is death.
>
> My days are numbered without my knowing it. I would like to die now—already—in the fullness of life—and after death remember for the rest of my life.
>
> Thinking about it, what we understand of death that frightens us and causes our fear, is seeing how it is necessary to die.
>
> God acted on a large scale. To do this he wasn't concerned with individual or even with collective death.
>
> He only works with millennia. Minutes don't count for Him. He reaches the inevitable through thousands of centuries. And we—we have a little flame of life that lights up and dies out. We must

grow up counting on the fact that we are the tiniest particle of Great Time That Does Not End.

God created death and afterward he could never repair it or abolish it. . . .

Death exists. Perhaps my ultimate destiny will be as an oboe.[23]

The desire to die is the desire to know; it is not the desire to disappear, and it is not suicide; it is the desire to enjoy.

As Kafka said:

"You keep on talking about death, and yet you do not die." "And yet I shall die. I am just saying my swan-song. One man's song is longer, another man's song is shorter. But the difference can never be more than a matter of a few words." [24]

This is our inner discourse. We have to be two to say that to ourselves: I the living one and I the dying one. Human beings desire this paradoxical duplicity, which decently shouldn't be expressed, which people like Kafka and Clarice express. There is an absolute difference between me and the dying one. But the author wants to die. Because it is over there that "it" happens. He or she envies, he or she is jealous, he or she loves the dying and the dead. It's a desire I have had to formulate for myself less clearly than Kafka did. I have never said to myself: What, you're not dying? Because I don't believe I am going to die. Why don't I, H.C., die and why does he die? One of us shall die. *I* don't die because you are the dead one. This is my life schema. Kafka's father was such that Kafka could say: I'm the one who will die. Mine, such that I can only say: why not me?

So, after all, the desire to die is only the desire to taste the fruits of the tree of Good and Evil. To be able to want to taste the fruits of the tree of Good and Evil, contrary to what the Bible says, one has to be mortal. It's very difficult if one isn't mortal. Not everyone is mortal. Not everyone has this difficult fortune. I myself don't have it.

I have always loved the writers whom I call writers of *extremity,* those who take themselves to the extremes of experience, thought, life.

The School of the Dead

When I began to read Clarice Lispector in 1977, I read her calmly and passionately in wonder. What I realize only now is that I read her—I'm forcing a bit, but not much, in order to reach a state of mind—beyond, outside time. She appeared so great and strong in her text that I didn't think of her outside it. I read her above and beyond Clarice Lispector. What carried me, what retained me, was the power of her thought. I spent a year listening to what she was saying, without thinking about her. It was all in the eternal future. And suddenly, I was told she had died. I believe this didn't affect me at all, because I hadn't thought of her as either alive or dead. The life and death of Clarice Lispector had remained in another world. I was in the future of Clarice Lispector's texts.

When I read Kafka, I read him dead, all the more dead because he died in the same way and at the same age as my father. So it was obvious to me: I didn't even wonder about it. I always read him as dead. He was dead. The dead man.

Once a dear friend of mine (a woman) had me read Thomas Bernhard. At first I felt a deep aversion (his). Then I enjoyed myself. I had never read texts that made me laugh, the most mysterious thing of all. I said to myself: How can you write something so impudent without paying for it?

I was delighted that he existed. One day my mother came in and said: "Have you heard, that man you are reading (I was reading *A Child* at the time), well, he just died." [25] His was also an early death. So I was laughing at the moment he died. You will tell me everyone dies, but not everyone dies of writing.

Here are two writers who died of writing because they went so far toward approaching what is forbidden, so near what Kafka called the fire, that they actually caught fire. In fact Clarice Lispector only barely escaped being burned alive ten years before she did eventually die. She was seriously burnt, her bed caught fire, and she was saved at the last moment by her son, but her hands were badly burned and she could no longer write by hand.

Ingeborg Bachmann, the great Austrian writer, died mysteriously in

1971. People keep saying they do not know what happened. Her bedroom, her bathroom, they say, suddenly burst into flames, and she died. One does not know whether she committed suicide, as is implied in biographical notes about her, or whether it was an accident. There is burning to death in her books. When you are alive and writing you question yourself: Am I writing? Am I burning? Or am I pretending? These writers have gone toward the truth.

(I hope you will forgive me if I use the word "truth." The moment I say "truth" I expect people to ask: "What is truth?" "Does truth exist?" Let us imagine that it exists. The word exists, therefore the feeling exists.)

Retrospectively, after long years of reading, I said to myself: when I read someone that person dies. But I can do nothing about it. I only like those who write from there. I am not a sorceress and I am innocent of these events and coincidences. On the other hand the fact that I have an ear for a certain type of writing that doesn't hesitate to go beyond the self, beyond oneself, is of my doing. These texts move me, touch me, strike me with blows of the axe because they are the texts Kafka talks about, texts that give me such intense joy that it resembles pain. And we can only undergo that joy *over there.* I could say "there"—it's the direction. These are people who write *in the direction.*

In the direction of truth, because telling the truth and dying go together. Something allies truth with death. We cannot bear to tell the truth, except in the final hour, at the last minute, since to do so earlier costs too much. But when does the last minute come?

Perhaps going in the direction of what we call truth is, at least, to "unlie," not to lie. Our lives are buildings made up of lies. We have to lie to live. But to write we must try to unlie. Something renders going in the direction of truth and dying almost synonymous. It is dangerous to go in the direction of truth. We cannot read about it, we cannot bear it, we cannot say it; all we can think is that only at the very last minute will you know what you are going to say, though we never know when the last minute will be.

Those I love go in the direction of what they call the last hour—what Clarice Lispector calls "the hour of the star," the hour of relinquishing all the lies that have helped us live.

Writing or saying the truth is equivalent to death, since we cannot tell the truth. It is in every way forbidden because it hurts everyone. We never say the truth, we must lie, mostly as a result of two needs: our need for love and cowardice. The cowardice of love but also love's courage. Cowardice and courage are so close that they are often exchanged. Cowardice is probably the strange, tortuous path of courage. Love is tortuous. So it is only at the very last page of a book that we perhaps get a chance to say what we have never said, write what we have never written all our lives, i.e., the most precarious, the best, in other words, the worst.

I have respect and admiration for those writers who, in their lifetime, have approached that point where cowardice and courage are so close to each other they might fly into the flames if they were to say one word more. This is what Tsvetaeva describes, the point that I call the truth and which she calls the magical words in writing. She alludes to a short episode in Pushkin's *The Captain's Daughter* in a small text called "Pushkin and Pugachev." Pushkin's novel starts with the hero, Grinov, as a young boy aged sixteen. He is going to meet Pugachev, an imposter, a Cossack who challenged the Czar's power and almost became the Russian emperor. At the beginning of the novel, young Grinov gets lost in a huge snowstorm, and suddenly, in the distance he sees something moving. Tsvetaeva cites this episode:

> It is strange that I, who was so slow at reasoning and so bad at guessing in childhood, and in life too, I whom it was so easy to fool, guessed right in this instance and right away, as soon as amid *the murky maelstrom of the blizzard* something black could be seen. Right away I was on guard, knowing, knowing, knowing, that it was not "a stump nor a wolf" but that one thing.
>
> And when the unknown object started moving toward us and in two minutes became a man, I already knew that it was not a "good

> man," as the coachman called him but a bad man, the bogey-man, that man.
>
> The unknown thing was—the very best known thing.
>
> I had waited for the Pathfinder my whole life long, my whole huge seven-year-old life.
>
> It was the thing that waits for us at every turn of the road and of the corridor, that comes out from behind every clump of the forest and every corner of the street: the miracle into which the child and the poet walk without thinking as if walking home, that one and only walk homeward that we have, for which we give up—all our family homes![26]

That is the definition of truth, it is the thing you must not say. "The miracle into which the child and the poet walk" as if walking home, and home is there. And for this home, this foreign home, about which we know nothing and which looks like a black thing moving, for this we give up all our family homes.

The thing that is both known and unknown, the most unknown and the best unknown, this is what we are looking for when we write. We go toward the best known unknown thing, where knowing and not knowing touch, where we hope we will know what is unknown. Where we hope we will not be afraid of understanding the incomprehensible, facing the invisible, hearing the inaudible, thinking the unthinkable, which is of course: thinking. Thinking is trying to think the unthinkable: thinking the thinkable is not worth the effort. Painting is trying to paint what you cannot paint and writing is writing what you cannot know before you have written: it is preknowing and not knowing, blindly, with words. It occurs at the point where blindness and light meet. Kafka says—one very small line lost in his writing—"to the depths, to the depths." Going to the depths is exactly what these people do—exactly what Dostoyevsky did in the last century.

But in this century if we fail it is because we are afraid. We do not succeed; yet books are exactly those steps that should lead us to the point where oppositions meet, and, coinciding, suddenly open up to what

Kafka would call "the Holy of the Holies." But, as you know, to set foot in the Holy of the Holies, you must take everything off.

> Before setting foot in the Holy of the Holies you must take off your shoes, yet not only your shoes, but everything; you must take off your travelling-garment and lay down your luggage; and under that you must shed your nakedness and everything that is under the nakedness and everything that hides beneath that, and then the core and the core of the core, then the remainder and then the residue and then even the Holy of the Holies and let yourself be absorbed by it; neither can resist the other.[27]

Ingeborg Bachmann took everything off.

I started reading Ingeborg Bachmann ten years ago but was unable to continue out of pain, and it was only recently that she came back to me. She was a friend of Celan's; when I first read Celan I did not see anyone around him. I read him as an isolated and chosen person. Then I read Nelly Sachs, then Thomas Bernhard, and gradually I realized that Ingeborg Bachmann had loved Nelly Sachs and had known her. Nelly Sachs and Celan had known each other. Ingeborg Bachmann knew Celan. She was Thomas Bernhard's friend. There was a burning thread of correspondence and love between these people, because they had the same type of personal and historical experience, an experience connected to fire and ashes.

This is what Ingeborg Bachmann says in the avant-propos of one of her short novels entitled *Der Fall Franza*.

> I have often wondered and you too [she says to the public], what has become of the virus of crime. It cannot suddenly twenty years ago have disappeared from the universe just because murder today is no longer encouraged and rewarded by medals. Of course, though massacres belong to the past, the assassins are still among us. [She is speaking of the Nazis here.] They are often recalled, sometimes they are even recognized and some of them are judged. We have been prompted to discover the assassins' existence not through re-

> ports in newspapers but through literature instead. Today it has become infinitely more difficult to commit crimes and this makes them more subtle so that we almost do not perceive them, we almost do not understand them even though they are committed daily around us and in our homes. [Indeed.] I affirm and I want to bring proof of it today that most human beings did not die but were murdered because there is nothing more monstrous than a human being, if you will allow me the schoollike tone I am using. For the crimes that require some spirit, that touch our spirit, touch us profoundly, blood is not poured and the massacre does not take place where we are used to seeing it. But crimes have not become fewer, they simply require more refinement and that is why they are more terrible.[28]

The question of the presence of *crime* in human beings has been put to us by the Austrian Ingeborg Bachmann in each of her texts. The same harsh anguish is echoed by the Brazilian Clarice Lispector.

The Passion According to G. H. is also the passion according to the cockroach G. H. almost puts to death. It is equally the passion according to the Woman or even to Women: the two characters who measure themselves against each other and exchange silent cries, repulsion, death instincts, are both females. One is a woman, G. H., and the other is a cockroach—in Brazilian, *barata*—which is feminine. G. H. meets the barata in a room where there is no one left in the world beyond herself and the barata. The barata embodies the whole history and the whole memory of the living universe. For G. H., it is the occasion to rethink the whole of human experience. Gradually she comes to the point where she thinks that to come to terms with the barata's existence she has to overcome repulsion, since this prevents her from communicating with other people: she must exchange in the deepest way, translated into concrete fact by her "courageous" decision to eat the barata. However, this is not the end of the story because Clarice Lispector is wiser. Once G. H. has actually tasted the barata she realizes that this is not the best way to come into contact with anyone. She discovers that eating the other, cannibalism, is not the wisest way to fight back repulsion after all. So she thinks onward. It is nonetheless through this act of symbolic and concrete violence that she learns to think further than the repulsion that is always at work in us. Through death, toward the recognition of love.

6. The Inclination for Avowal

I have talked about these authors who are dear to me. Why do I feel a certain joyful love for them? Because they all inspire me with a feeling that resembles Genet's feeling for his "Le Funambule": they inspire me with fear and admiration.[29] I feel fear and confidence. (In French I would use the masculine plural, *ils,* for *they* because I put Bernhard in this group, although most of these authors are women.) Because what they reveal is audaciousness, which *consists in saying the worst,* in writing the worst, making apparent, naming the worst. I am not talking about religious people; these are poets. It's not about confessing oneself. This fascinates me, because confession puts into play something which seems to me impossible and terrible: erasure. Are we supposed to be amnestied? Confession treats ritually what is absolutely untreatable.

It so happens that these authors emerged wounded and enraged from a scene of confession. Because there is no God in their texts, even though there may be some in their hearts. That's another thing. *There is no religion. There is the human.*

So, what these "people whose souls are already mature" do, as Clarice would say, is to venture there where we don't have the strength or the means to venture, to the edge of our abyss: and then to describe it.[30]

A POSSIVEIS LEITORES

> Este livro é como um livro qualquer. Mas eu ficaria contente se fosse lido apenas por pessoas de alma jà formada. Aquelas que sabem que a aproximaçao, do que quer que seja, se faz gradualemente e penosamente—atravessando inclusive o oposto daquilo de que se vai aproximar. Aquelas pessoas que, só elas, entenderao bem devagar que este livro nada tira de ninguém. A mim, por exemplo, o personagem G. H. foi dando pouco a pouco uma alegria dificil; mas chama-se alegria.
>
> C. L.[31]

TO POSSIBLE READERS

This book is like any other book. But I would be pleased if it were read only by people whose souls are already mature. Those who know that the approach to anything is done gradually and painfully—and includes as well passing through the opposite of what is being approached. These people and they alone will understand very slowly that this book takes nothing away from anyone. To me, for example, the character G. H. gradually gave a difficult joy; but it is called joy.

C. L.[32]

That's the path of "the maturing of the soul": go and see, and not only see but inscribe the abyss we are. Try to look for the worst in yourself and confide it where there is no process of erasure, where the worst remains the worst. Try to write the worst and you will see that the worst will turn against you and, treacherously, will try to veil the worst. For we cannot bear the worst. Writing the worst is an exercise that requires us to be stronger than ourselves. My authors have killed.

In *The Passion According to G. H.*, the crime is perpetrated on a cockroach. If I were to tell you the story of the cockroach's murder it would have no effect on you. Only inside the text, as we inhabit the text, do we tremble where Clarice wants us to tremble. It happens that I kill. My victim is a fly. It happens that when I write a fly enters: I try to chase it away; a combat begins. It happens that, having been unable to save the fly, I kill it. I admit this, then feel I have increased my share of the crime. I have killed flies and then there is no end to killing. Will I ever admit it? Never really.

I have the inclination for avowal. What would the opposite of need for avowal be? The need to remain silent. Does that exist? Do we really want secrets? Real need is on the side of avowal. The true secret causes the most suffering, because it is the exact figure of death. If we have a secret we don't tell then we truly are a tomb.

Thomas Bernhard is orgiastic in his avowal. The fact that human relations should be so intimately woven with the worst has always made him laugh. But it is Clarice Lispector who has said the strongest things about this tangling. This tangling in us, which we call "human," of Good with Evil: this taste of Good for Evil, of Love for Hatred. The dark, wild, good-bad part in us; the beast-part in human beings. In Clarice Lispector's pitiless works we sometimes measure ourselves and are measured against a being of our species—though one who is violently different from us—sometimes, as a woman, we are measured against a man, sometimes as a woman we are measured against a beggar, or against a blindman, or else against a hen, or against a barata; sometimes, as a man, we are measured against a dog. . . . Measured and weighed. We must at times go and look for either the worst or *the best* of ourselves in a purer, more naked being than we are.

A woman whom a man did not want to love went to a zoo to seek what she wasn't able to find in herself: the source, the secret of hatred. This incident occurs in a short story entitled "The Buffalo." [33] There is a bitter unknown substance that circulates in us and that is called "hatred." For the woman in the story it is a question of having this substance crystalize, coagulate. It's a matter of recognizing it, seizing it, probing its nature, enjoying it. What does this substance that impassions and poisons consist of? "The Buffalo" tells us in a mortal way. The need for avowal is the need to spit out, vomit, reject a certain substance—which is part of me.

Here, a woman silently asks a buffalo's brutality the secret of all brutality.

In another story, a "man" asks a dog for our most profoundly buried secret, the secret that is blended with human nature itself. It concerns love, which is not what we think it is, we who think that love loves and that we love to love. We who believe we know, we who calculate, we who are kinds of "mathematics professors." The story is entitled "The Crime of the Mathematics Professor." [34] But in the narrative there is no titular "Professor." There is only "Man." Without a name, without a profession. Man-humanity, the one who makes decisions in the family, this is "Man." "Man" arrives at the top of a mountain, driven by a mysterious scheme. Man has glasses. The glasses are more than just glasses. To "see" better Man takes his glasses off. The text doesn't stop taking off and putting the glasses back on again, always in a subtle counterbalance or contra tempo. This is how we regulate our way of not seeing, or seeing what we don't want to see. Seeing, not seeing, making visible, hiding/exposing, what? What is there in that heavy bag he is carrying?

Man opens the sack and pulls out a dead and unknown dog: very unknown, very dead. "The dead dog." Now we will bury it. Is it about the dog's burial? Man thinks and calculates. Calculates the precise details of the burial up here beneath the sky—who sees or doesn't see?—thinks "about the real dog." Suddenly we learn that the real dog lives in another town while here Man is burying it on the mountain top, in the guise of another dog, the one that is dead. Double burial, of the living and the dead. For it seems that what is urgent is *to bury*. . . .

We need dogs. This is why in our favorite books there are so many dogs who are us; Kafka's dogs; or cats; Edgar Allan Poe's cats.

. . . Man wants to bury the dog exactly where he himself would like to be buried, he, Man, if he were dead. We/he must bury. We constantly believe we must repress, forget and bury. Yet this isn't true. The desire to bury hides a much more twisted desire: Man wants to *be seen burying*—wants to be discovered in the middle of hiding. (So who sees him up there burying? No one. . . .) Man only half-buries the dog. In fact, he exhibits the burial in such a way it seems like a disinterment.

He must unbury the burying, which is equivalent to bringing what has been repressed back to the surface of consciousness. Clarice Lispector never speaks in terms of psychoanalysis, however, but in terms of her own ethics. Man has to do this because he felt compelled to abandon the dog that is alive. This is a crime. Yet this crime is unfortunately invisible. Man is concerned with the crime, which, though it exists, has not happened, making him guilty although he is not guilty. Man cannot bear having committed what I would call *a perfect crime,* since no one knows about it. Even the dog does not know about it. The crime is so perfect it is imperfect. The really perfect crime should indeed be imperfect. But this crime, perpetrated on a dog, is not recognized as a crime, and this is what Man must deal with. We are criminals and we do not know how to express or prove that we are criminals. The problem is that if, as criminals, we were recognized as such, we would have to pay for the crime. Yet if we paid, the crime would disappear and our debt would be wiped out. We must keep our crime in order to keep our crime safe, to avoid the terrible fate of being forgiven. That is: how do we save our crime from the punishment and thus the forgiveness that threaten to wipe out our crime? How do we escape the burial of the fault that deprives us of our truth? It is difficult, almost impossible, as Clarice Lispector shows in her extraordinary story. What finally emerges from the earth of the narrative is that *we need the scene of the crime* in order to come to terms with ourselves: we need the theater of the crime. We need to be able to expose the crime and at the same time to somehow keep it alive.

The inclination for avowal, the desire for avowal, the yearning to taste the taste of avowal, is what compels us to write: both the need to avow and its impossibility. Because most of the time the moment we avow we fall into the snare of atonement: confession—and forgetfulness. Confession is the worst thing: it disavows what it avows.

How do we avow the unavowable? This is the problem the narration, the point of enunciation deals with in Edgar Allan Poe's "The Black Cat."

The Story of the Black Id. [35]

It's about a man who tells an appalling story. He has had a wonderful childhood and a tender relation to the world of animals. As an adult he is very happy. His wife, who wishes to please him, brings cats, dogs, fish, etc., into the house . . . and a black cat. This cat is called Pluto. Suddenly, the story turns round. The cat is a turning point, a stroke of genius from Poe. The man takes to drink. We don't know why. Is the cat Evil? The man's character alters. He becomes capable of violence and cruelty. The cat is so impassioned, it never lets the narrator out of paw's reach. One day, exasperated by love, the narrator catches Pluto and pokes out one of its eyes with a knife. After this he sleeps himself sober. The cat recovers. Henceforth there is ambivalence between the narrator and cat.

The narrator ends up killing Pluto:

> It was this unfathomable longing of the soul *to vex itself*—to offer violence to its own nature—to do wrong for wrong's sake only—that urged me to continue and finally to consummate the injury I had inflicted upon the unoffending brute. One morning, in cold blood, I slipped a noose about its neck and hung it to the limb of a tree;—hung it with the tears streaming from my eyes, and with the bitterest remorse at my heart;—hung it *because* I knew that it had loved me, and *because* I felt it had given me no reason of offence;—hung it *because* I knew that in so doing I was committing a sin—a deadly sin that would so jeopardize my immortal soul as to place it—if such a thing were possible—even beyond the reach of the infinite mercy of the Most Merciful and Most Terrible God.[36]

A second cat arrives. In an inn where he is getting drunk the man sees a black spot on the shelf (this makes us think of the black spot in *My Pushkin*, which turns out to be Pugachev and about whom Tsvetaeva says: *I had waited for the Pathfinder my whole life long.*[37] A black spot in the background of the picture, the black man, bearer of death, whom I love).

When the man approaches the black spot, it is a cat exactly like Pluto except that it has a white patch on its chest. The cat follows the man home; and the story begins again. The second cat will be drawn into the story of the first cat; the narrator once again shows the same reactions, although in a displaced manner. He starts to have a horror of this cat as the same cat. Hatred develops. The memory of the first scene reminds him of what it cost him in feelings of ambivalence and terror. Little by little the narrator's impulse grows. He ends up calling the cat a monster. The story ends with the immurement of corpses in the cellar. One day the narrator goes down to the cellar with his wife and the cat. The characters cannot be distinguished. The cat slips between the narrator's legs who swings an axe at the cat. The cat is quicker than he is and the axe falls on his wife, cutting her in two. It is at this point that the narrator undertakes the corpse's immurement. The man is in his cellar; he considers every possiblity. He works intensely. All this man's libidinal energy is invested in the task. He tears down a section of the wall and immures his wife. We, the readers, follow every minute detail of the proceedings. At times we are at the level of realism, at times in metaphor; we are repeating our own way of immuring—not a corpse: but its equivalent. We too manage to bury to perfection. This is our great desire.

The narrative is *in the first person.* I screened that when I told you the story. This is how far Poe is able to go: he could write that *only in the first person.* Had he written it in the second or third person, it would have introduced a distancing dimension, and we would have swooped down on the possibility of not having to believe, of not feeling touched.

But we read as the first person. It's a question of who constitutes the narrative. Poe creates a narration within the narration, but there is also an invisible element not printed in the book that says: And you, what have you immured? What is your story?

The whole text works like lava covering everything up, it functions as a constant immurement. From the start the adult represses and immures his golden childhood. Just as one act covers another, one cat covers another, there is a succession of increasingly violent episodes up to the end of the narrative. We too are subject to this escalation of violence created by one violent act covering another. The tragedy of violence is that it erases its own violent degrees, so that we may erase the first act of violence as trifling even though it was decisive. All violence has a history. When we arrive at a certain degree of subjective, phantasmic, or sociopolitical violence it both reproduces secondary violence and creates new violence.

This mechanism of immurement plays on two levels: the symbolic one of putting the immurement of repressions and amnesia into concrete form and the concrete immurement that takes place in the cellar. The narrator ends up closing himself in the depths of the unconscious and his own house, the one serving as the figure for the other.

Approaching the place where we will expose the crime that is part of our soul is difficult. We want to know the taste of avowal, which is joyful, yet at the same time we come into contact with something we are afraid of: hatred. We who are as full of hatred as we are of love, since hatred is a part of love; we who want to throw up the substance of hatred but to know at the same time what love is made of.

We need dogs to understand this strange, ambivalent relation we have to love—hatred. I don't have a dog. I avoid having a dog. I have always been aware that I have avoided having dogs. A dog is a threat. What is threatening about dogs is their terrible love. You learn this the moment you see a particular dog. Some dogs are like human beings, full of hatred, but most dogs are bundles of love. This infinite, complete, and limitless giving of love is exhausting for a human being. We are a mixture of love and its contrary. Apparently there is no such mixture in a dog's love. Poe wrote "The Black Cat" about this: a cat's love that is so infinite the narrator comes to hate the cat.

Meeting a dog you suddenly see the abyss of love. Such limitless love doesn't fit our economy. We cannot cope with such an open, superhuman relation.

7. Toward the Last Hour

How can we keep our mixture of innocence and crime sufficiently alive and open to live and write? How can we proceed to the burning point, reach that *last hour*, when we'll be able to write or say everything we have never dared say out of love and cowardice?

What would happen if we were able to reach this hour of grace is that we would perhaps be able to say what we have never said. Dying without having done so: that's what death is. Why do we desire to die so much? Because we desire to say so much. Why do we so desire to attain this mysterious moment? Because we desire to live as we have never lived, totally nude. At this moment, if we have worked on the way—because it's an enormous task to belie and unlie—we might say everything that, out of love and cowardice, out of love as cowardice, we would never have said.

Everything we could never have said, but have read, since at least it's written. We have shivered reading tales of crime, it's us, though under an assumed name, under a pseudonym: which is why we don't recognize ourselves or flee the texts that know us.

The cemetery scene, Thomas Bernhard's scene in Traunstein, is beyond our strength; it is not that it is simply forbidden us, it is forbidden almost from the beginning. This is already true of our own personal stories: provided they are told by fearless narrators, each human being's story is always the greatest and cruelest of stories. We are the ones who reduce and annihilate them to nothing. Otherwise, every day, we are characters (returning and reappearing) from the great tragedies we love to reread—from the tragedies and myths, and also from somewhere far away, in the neighborhood of the child's bedroom, from cruel children's tales that we enormously enjoy even though they are tales of a juvenile age. We are full of ogres. As we grow up we are in "King Lear," we may go as far as "Titus Andronicus," we are in "Othello"; we are in all the Greek tragedies, which are our tragedies, except that we are not encouraged to make the connection: acting as though we weren't the characters in smaller or greater tragedies.

8. We Need the Scene of the Crime

We have not told the truth about what I have called *the worst,* though the secret of the worst is often not much: we are the ones who make it worse. This "thing" produces effects of death between individuals. I am not adopting Ingeborg Bachmann's statement, which I hear with tenderness, sympathy, and sorrow. I am not at the point where I could rightly call the relationship between men and women fascist. It was true for her: the relationship between men and women of her time, in Austria, was dressed and presented in the suit of fascism.

It's only at the end—all of Ingeborg Bachmann's books are books about the end—she writes each time in agony—that everything we weren't able to say will be said. Not only is there a war between people, but this war is produced by sexual difference. And not just by sexual difference. By the wiles, paradoxes, and surprises that sexual difference reserves for us. This is why the man-woman conflict is insufficient for me, in my time, in my place. It *is* a question of sexual difference, only sexual difference isn't what we think it is. It's both tortuous and complicated. There is sexual difference, and there is what it becomes in its appearances and distributions in each one of us. We already knew it with Shakespeare: ourselves we do not owe and we do not know whom we love. Before the final hour we will not be able to say that such and such a woman was a man. Why can't we say it? Because it would be saying what the world is not yet ready to hear. Besides, it's dangerous, since we are on the way toward what could be retaken and distorted by misogyny. Let's imagine we love a woman who is a man inside. This means we love not a man exactly, but a woman who is a man, which is not quite the same thing: it's a woman who is also a man, another species. These complexities are not yet audible. Although this is true, strangely enough we are still today at a clear-cut difference, we continue to say man and woman even though it doesn't work. We are not made to reveal to what extent we are complex. We are not strong enough, not agile enough; only writing is able to do this. Sometimes we are married to a man because he is a woman, even though we believed we had married a man. Whom have we married? Our grandmother perhaps. A woman who was the replica of a woman-eating man passed off in the world as a woman par excellence. In this guise she slaughtered women wholesale, while being extolled by men for her maternal charm. This is a true tale. We should write "The Fables of Sexual Difference." They should be the tales of our times; they would be staggering. The Greeks did it. In the Greek tragedies Aeschylus tells us right away that Clytemnestra is of virile strength. But then who kills Agamemnon? I'd like to know. Is it a man or a woman who kills Agamemnon? Does it mean that a woman who kills a man is a man, etc.? In other words, that only a man kills a man. But then why accuse Clytemnestra of being a woman? There's no end to it. . . .

We could think over these mysteries but we don't. We are unable to inscribe or write them since we don't know who we are, something we never consider since we always take ourselves for ourselves; and from this point on we no longer know anything. I'll tell you frankly that I haven't the faintest idea who I am, but at least I know I don't know. I am not the other able to perceive me. I know some things about myself. I know who I'm not, I believe.

As for you, the other, I am where I think you are not who you believe yourself to be, who you seem to be, who the world believes you to be—I am using the second person to avoid the difficulty of speaking either in the masculine or the feminine—on the other hand, given that the definition of me or you is the most vulnerable thing in us, this prevents me from thinking what I think. When we say to a woman that she is a man or to a man that he is a woman, it's a terrible insult. This is why we cut one another's throats.

We have extremely strong identifications, which found our house. An identity card doesn't allow for confusion, torment, or bewilderment. It asserts the simplified and clear-cut images of conjugality. If the truth about loving or hateful choices were revealed it would break open the earth's crust. Which is why we live in legalized and general delusion. Fiction takes the place of reality. This is why simply naming one of these turns of the unconscious that are part of our strange human adventure engenders such upsets (which are at once intimate, individual, and political); why consciously or unconsciously we constantly try to save ourselves from this naming. The one whom a woman calls "husband," is he the father, the son, or the he-mother? The one who governs the country, is he father or son? The war that divides the world in two halves is a war between father and son, or else a war between the archaic father, i.e., a type of mother and the jealous son. And what about women?

In our impassioned times on all political fronts, where it is largely a question of an open and covert struggle with the mysteries of sexual difference, as women we are at the *obligatory* mercy of simplifications. In order to defend women we are obliged to speak in the feminist terms of "man" and "woman." If we start to say that such and such a woman is perhaps not entirely a woman or not a woman at all, that this "father" is not a father, we can no longer fight since we no longer know who is in front of us. It's so destructive, so destabilizing that those of us who are conscious of what is at stake are often pushed toward a form of interdict. Only when we are posthumous can we place the earth in question; make the earth tremble.

My characters—Clarice, Ingeborg Bachmann, Kafka, Dostoyevsky, Thomas Bernhard, Marina Tsvetaeva—did this in their writing. Why did I begin to love Tsvetaeva so much? Because she wrote in the thirties that she was born from Pushkin's belly. And yet knowing too much too soon can lead to the tree from which one hangs oneself, because one is too alone.

These are people who went through the storm evoked by Tsvetaeva at the beginning of *My Pushkin* and that blows in the opening scene of *The Captain's Daughter*. This turbulent landscape is our inner storm, it's the curtain-raising of the unconscious. The world is white, we are lost, a great wind blows, and there in the background is a small black spot. We wonder what it is.

These people have taken us through the storm "toward the depths" where we can't see clearly what we see, to discover "the most known unknown thing."

This most known unknown thing will become for Pushkin and Tsvetaeva a marvelous and strange character who *in reality* was Pugachev, the impostor, and who *in truth* is the typical character of our secret scene, the person who loves us and who kills us. Loving and killing absolutely cannot be disentangled. The only person who can kill us is clearly the person who loves us and whom we love.

Our pathfinders—Tsvetaeva says she immediately fell in love with the word "pathfinder"—take us this way, where we will be both spectators and actors of the scene of the crime. Only poetically and in the imaginary can we approach these places of fire.

We are all dog-killers of the dog you are, killers of others. It is simply a question of designating the scene or scenes of *abandonment* that punctuate our paths so that they may be envisioned. We are abandoned and we abandon. Clarice's Man says to his dog, who is no longer there: "you immediately became an abandonable being."

When do we reach the hour when we say we have deceived everyone in our lives in order to keep what we call life going? I don't know. We go to the School of the Dead to hear a little of what we are unable to say. This is why we need the books that hurt us. But often we are in the situation that Kafka describes in the passage entitled "On Suspended Animation," in which he tells of the experience of going to the other side, of Moses on Sinai, of people who have apparently died and then returned.[38] And of those who apparently died and then revived not one of them said a word about their experience, although we would like to know what happened.

Writing is the delicate, difficult, and dangerous means of succeeding in avowing the unavowable. Are we capable of it? This is my desire. I too would like to die; though this doesn't mean I have succeeded. I make the effort. So far I haven't succeeded. In the meantime, I do the closest thing I can. To approach the place where I can unlie and have something in common—as Clarice dreams—with the dying, I go to the other school, the nearest one, the one that most resembles the School of the Dead: the School of Dreams.

Tomorrow, tonight, we who are unfortunately immortal will go to the School of Dreams.

The School of Dreams

- The Dream Teaches Us "The Pure Element of Fear"

- How Can We Finish a Book, a Dream?

- I Like Dream Writers

- The History of My Dreams

- Voyage to the Nearest Dreams

- What Must We Do To Get to the School of Dreams?

I'll take up my axe again. We'll clear a trail through the forest. Moving forward in the axe's light.

I'm rewriting my H. My ladder of writing.

The School of Dreams? How to get there? We can't go via the city, nor at will, nor by bus.

The question as to whether we know we can go to the School of Dreams is always formidable. There is something in the title "The

School of Dreams" that plays with us: a type of displaced game of cat and mouse. Let's suppose that the mouse has a great desire to be eaten. Going to the School of Dreams trifles with us.

Dreams await us in a country we can't get tickets to. If I say: I want to go to the School of Dreams, there's every chance the dreams will say to me: you've got another thing coming, without my ever reaching the dreams.

Today I made two Freudian slips: I forgot to bring two texts, *The Interpretation of Dreams* and, in *Mandelstam: The Complete Critical Prose and Letters,* a text entitled "I don't read." [1] Perhaps at the School of Dreams we also work with lack, absence, and omission. But I didn't forget *O Lustro* by Clarice Lispector.[2] Here's a book "I read" but haven't finished reading. I don't make an effort either to read it or not read it. I let it be, it's in the room where I am, often I don't read it and during this time it beams obscurely. It's a form of reading. (This is how we get to the School of Dreams, by making a vast detour.) There is something extraordinary in our relationship with books. The book is the Door—the Dream of the other that doesn't escape us—that dreams us and waits for us. What is magnificent about books is that they can wait for us. This is how *O Lustro* waits for me, and I am in no hurry. It gives me time. This is one of the mysteries of writing. Not all books give us time. *O Lustro* gives time because it is itself carved from time, it is so rich, thick, so well-thumbed that it is pure writing substance. It doesn't tell a story. It makes us feel, taste, touch life. It is there like an immobile, eternal, complete person whose never-failing characteristic is to produce something continually strange: *patience,* despite or with desire. I haven't finished reading *O Lustro.* I am in the process of reading it, and this "in the process of" includes passages of nonreading through which the book continues to emit its beams.

It's the same for *Mandelstam: The Complete Critical Prose and Letters.* To me, these two books represent the two poles of writing.

There is no greater *reader* than Mandelstam. Most poets read on the sly, barely give themselves to reading, whereas Mandelstam is a sublime reader for whom we must raise reading to the height of poetry, making it an equivalent art.

Let us refer again to the first sentences of Kafka's letter (cf. p. 17). Here's the secret:

> I think we ought to read only the kind of books that wound and stab us. If the book we are reading doesn't wake us up with a blow on the head, what are we reading it for?[3]

Whoever wants to write must be able to reach this lightening region that takes your breath away, where you *instantaneously* feel at sea and where the moorings are severed with the already-written, the already-known. This "blow on the head" that Kafka describes is the blow on the head of the deadman/deadwoman we are. And that is the awakening from the dead.

I can't make a recipe of it, for as soon as we begin to inscribe signs, to attract attention, we destroy. So though you should hear everything I say, it should then be absorbed, pass through the blood, without your *thinking* about it, with your living it.

All great texts begin in this manner that *breaks:* they break with our thought habits, with the world around us, in an extreme violence that is due to rapidity. They hurl us off to foreign countries. The beginning of this text by Mandelstam is the absolute lesson:

> Grass on the street of Petersbourg—the first sprouts of the virgin forest that will cover the site of modern cities. This bright tender verdure, astonishing in its freshness, belongs to a new inspired nature.[4]

◧

Not everyone is given access to this other world where the dead and the dying live. We are not all guests of the dead, this wisest of companies. If we can't get there by dying, then let's go there by dreaming.

One of Kafka's Dreams

> I was a visitor among the dead. It was a large, clean vault, there were some coffins there, but there was still plenty of room, two coffins were open, inside they looked like rumpled beds from which people had just got up. A desk stood a little to one side, so that I did not notice it at once, a man of powerful build sat at it. In his right hand he held a pen, it was as though he had been writing and had only just stopped, his left hand was toying with a shining watch-chain on his waistcoat and his head was bent low toward it. A charwoman was sweeping the place, but there was nothing to be swept up.[5]

This dream continues for a long time, and what Kafka is telling us is a whole adventure, an entire life among the dead. Let's follow him:

> On Suspended Animation
>
> Anyone who has once been in a state of suspended animation can tell terrible stories about it, but he cannot say what it is like after death, he has been actually no nearer to death than anyone else, fundamentally he has only "lived" through an extraordinary experience, and not-extraordinary, everyday life has become more valuable to him as a result. It is similar with everyone who has experienced something extraordinary. For instance Moses certainly experienced something extraordinary on Mount Sinai, but instead of submitting to this extraordinary experience, like someone in a state of suspended animation, not answering and remaining quiet in his coffin, he fled down the mountain and, of course, had valuable things to tell, and loved, even more than before, the people to whom he had fled and then sacrificed his life for them, one might say: in gratitude. From both, however, from those who have returned from a state of suspended animation and from Moses, who returned, one can learn a great deal, but the decisive thing cannot be discovered from them, for they themselves have not discovered (it). If they had discovered it, they would not have come back at all. But we do not even want to discover it. This can be shown by the fact that

> we may occasionally, for instance, have the wish to experience the experience of the man in a state of suspended animation, or Moses' experience, so long as the return is guaranteed, to undergo it as it were with a "safe-conduct," indeed, we may even wish death for ourselves, but not even in our thoughts should we wish to be alive and in the coffin without any chance of return, or to remain on Mount Sinai.[6]

This text has always fascinated me: it evokes the phenomenon of the state of indecision in which we don't know whether a person is alive or dead, though we assume they are dead. What Kafka is telling us here is both extremely important and, at the same time, marks our limits.

He is telling us in a complex way about our inability to desire what we desire—the secret. Our difficulty and our inability. We are not capable of becoming citizens of the other side: we prefer to die on this side rather than the other; which is what happens to Moses, as he comically says. Once on the mountain Moses had only one idea: to come running back down among the humans, even to the extent of sacrificing his life for them—the very life he did not dare lose up there.

What can be done to bring us closer to a place where the doors open and allow us to pass over to the other side: as Clarice says in *O Lustro,* "go beyond the limits of her life"?[7]

We can hope to move closer to everything we can't say without dying of fright through the School of Dreams. What makes us flee, what makes us come running down the mountain, what no man, no prophet could ever do, is *look straight at God,* look him in the eye. This is a metaphor. It's looking at what must not be looked at, at what would prevent us from existing, from continuing our ordinary, domestic lives, and what I call, for better or worse: "the truth."

Who (What) Does Not Regard Us / None of Our Business

This is what Clarice Lispector tells us about in a text called "Love," in which a woman, Ana, is accidentally surrendered to the face of God during an extraordinarily eloquent episode.[8] Ana is in a bus, she is carrying a shopping basket, she has all the distinguishing marks of the housewife, there are eggs in her basket, and in Ana's head, which is like a basket full of eggs, are the eggs of her life; during the day, she contemplates her life over a low heat: she has everything she should, her husband, her children, furniture, etc. At this moment, without meaning to, she sees the face of God, in an instantaneous, unbearable, admirable vision: that is, *she sees a blind man* on the edge of the sidewalk, and this makes the eggs explode. She sees (here it's even more complex) a blind man who is not only blind but who also chews. This is the secret of this powerful yet light scene: the blind man is chewing.

The blind man: the one who doesn't see us looking at him. We who are the looked-ats. We who live, eat, desire as we are looked upon. We who are looked-at lookers. But who never see ourselves as we are looked at, nor as we are seen. We who don't know we are blind and chewing.

> Suddenly she saw the man stationary at the tram stop. The difference between him and the others was that he was stationary. He stood with his hands held out in front of him—blind.
>
> But what else was there about him that made Ana sit up in distrust? Something disquieting was happening. Then she discovered what it was: the blind man was chewing gum . . . a blind man chewing gum. Anna still had time to reflect for a second that her brothers were coming to dinner—her heart pounding at regular intervals. Leaning forward, she studied the blind man intently, as one observes something incapable of returning our gaze. Relaxed, and with open eyes, he was chewing gum in the failing light. The facial movements of his chewing made him appear to smile then suddenly stop smiling, to smile and stop smiling. Ana stared at him as if he had insulted her. And anyone watching would have received the impression of a woman filled with hatred.[9]

I'll let you reflect on what is revealed in this passage, what in a flash deals such a blow, what strikes Ana, what makes the axe's blade inevitably fall. . . . This is what it is: Ana sees the face of God. You can die from it. You can also survive. Ana is wounded, split open. At the end of the text, she recloses what has been opened. But this might not have been reclosed. In another short story, "The Imitation of the Rose," the character doesn't close back up again.[10]

Staring at Length at the Face of God

What we hope for at the School of Dreams is the strength both to deal and to receive the axe's blow, to look straight at the face of God, *which is none other than my own face,* but seen naked, the face of my soul. The face of "God" is the unveiling, the staggering vision of the construction we are, the tiny and great lies, the small nontruths we must have incessantly woven to be able to prepare our brothers' dinner and cook for our children. An unveiling that only happens by surprise, by accident, and with a brutality that shatters: under the blow of the truth, the eggshell we are breaks. Right in the middle of life's path: the apocalypse; we lose a life.

To my sincere surprise, which is only the product of a form of blindness, I realized in time that the writers I love above all are of the dying-clairvoyant kind. What also reunites these authors is that they wrote, as I like to say, *by the light of the axe:* they all dared to write the worst, dared to "shatter the frozen sea," as Kafka puts it, break eggshells, the hulls of boats; they all dared to crack skulls, their own skulls, and return to the forest. All these things are discharged through violent separation, loss, and sudden good-luck—without which we would indeed be limited; we are able to do this at the School of Dreams. Where is it situated?

The School of the Dead is behind the wall.

The School of Dreams is Located Under the Bed

I have a faint recollection from an apparently naïve *Grimm's Tale* of a king whose daughters were ruining him. He kept them carefully locked in, as is proper, and didn't know why each day they needed to change their shoes. The daughters mysteriously wore out their shoes. Up until the day the king planted a spy to throw light on this matter. At nightfall the daughters pulled the bed aside, lifted up the trap door, climbed down the ladder beneath the palace, and went out into the forest and danced all night. Perhaps my version is not completely accurate, but that is of no importance, since it's the perfect metaphor for the School of Dreams, bringing together all the elements, including jouissance. It's about doing what is forbidden: sexual pleasure. There is also the wearing out of the shoes, which gave me particular pleasure when I was little without my knowing why. Now I know much better why and I dedicate this tale to Mandelstam.

Mandelstam asks very seriously in his "Conversation about Dante": how many pairs of shoes Dante must have worn out in order to write *The Divine Comedy,* because, he tells us, that could only have been written on foot, walking without stopping, which is also how Mandelstam wrote.[11] Mandelstam's whole body was in action, taking part, searching. Walking, dancing, pleasure: these accompany the poetic act. I wonder what kind of poet doesn't wear out their shoes, writes with their head. The true poet is a traveler. Poetry is about traveling on foot and all its substitutes, all forms of transportation.

Mandelstam wore out hundreds of pairs of shoes. You cannot write such intense, dense poetry without the kind of dance that dances you round the world. Mandelstam himself could not write without walking round and round. When he was prevented from walking he died.

So perhaps dreaming and writing do have to do with traversing the forest, journeying through the world, using all the available means of transport, using your own body as a form of transport. *The Wanderer,* a beautiful text by Hofmannsthal, tells the story of a journey through Greek and Turkish lands in which the narrator meets a strange traveler.[12] This man has apparently been walking for centuries, he is never named, but when you have lived in the country of poets, you immediately recognize who he is: he is Rimbaud. To meet Rimbaud we have to walk to Austria, to the Greece that is hidden within Austria; we have to travel to the heart of the country of the unconscious, where we may again find those countries we have lost, including Algeria and the Jardin d'Essais. But for this we have to walk, to use our whole body to enable the world to become flesh, exactly as this happens in our dreams. In dreams and writing our body is alive: we either use the whole of it or, depending on the dream, a part. We must embark on a body-to-body journey in order to discover the body.

In "*Love*" the event is inscribed by means of transport. Ana is transported, she is on the tracks, in a tram, and this means of transport is an element of immobility: the tram carries her, she doesn't move, and in front of her she sees the perfectly immobile blindman. It has to do with displacement.

In order to go to the School of Dreams, something must be displaced, starting with the bed. One has to get going. This is what writing is, starting off. It has to do with activity and passivity. This does not mean one will get there. Writing is not arriving; most of the time it's *not arriving*. One must go on foot, with the body. One has to go away, leave the self. How far must one not arrive in order to write, how far must one wander and wear out and have pleasure? One must walk as far as the night. One's own night. Walking through the self toward the dark.

■

Dreaming in 1990

My son is no bigger than a grub. This is why we almost forget him, we don't really believe in him, my dream and I. Where does he live? At the moment, between the leaves of a book. This is where he runs the least risk of being lost. Inversely, he risks being squashed, if someone puts something on the book. Otherwise he rests between the leaves without much difficulty. What is the future for such a grub? Not much hope. He'll vegetate. If he stays this size. But then he slowly takes on substance. This is doubtless the result of my efforts:

sometimes I take him out, I place him on a bed, or outside, for after all he has a right to the world, and he seems to lean toward life. The danger that someone unaware will crush him remains. Little by little he even gains in intelligence. He begins to think, to be happy, to become a real living being. Obviously, he is very far behind, since he has existed in this form for months. But now he has really decided to catch up. Now I spy him running, having gone downstairs, and climbing on dangerous edges. I am worried because he doesn't know what danger is.

I feel happiness, love for my grub leaving his twilight state. Seeing life "crystallize" is such a blessing. Suddenly, it's the descent between rough red boulders, in an invisible "taxi" that turns in circles several times in the circus of boulders, as if there were no way out. But in fact there is one.

Here is the portrait of my first written dream.

I'll return via my ladder to the first dream of dreams, the one everyone knows—except those who are not of Judeo-Christian culture, that is—Jacob's dream. At the beginning of this story, there is the whole matter of Jacob's genealogy. There are the two brothers, Jacob and Esau, and the father Isaac, the son of Abraham. Let's imagine we are the young Jacob. The parental genealogy provides a background. Stemming from Abraham we are constantly in the space where Good and Evil are infinitely tangled. Violent events are strewn through the characters' biographies. Then, as in a novel, we come to the small Isaac we left on the mountain, we progress through the story, and find a completely different Isaac. The Bible, like the dream, always brings us the violent sense of generations. We live bizarrely clinging to the level of our age, often with a vast repression of what has preceded us: we almost always take ourselves for the person we are at the moment we are at in our lives. What we don't know how to do is to think—it's exactly the same as for death—about what is in store for us. We don't know how to think about age; we are afraid of it and we repress it.

Writing has as its horizon this possibility, prompting us to explore all ages. Most poets are saved children: they are people who have kept their childhood alive and absolutely present. But the most difficult thing for human beings to do is to think ahead, to put ourselves in the shoes of those we have not yet been. Hence our difficulty in thinking over what is parked behind the so-called Golden Age barrier. What the Bible does for us is to make us live all along the generation ladder. With the Bible, we climb up and down through generations. The baby we picked up yesterday in the dust is now, in the next chapter, a tottering blindman. The one who is going to dream this well-known dream is the special son of a blind father, a most unusual man. There is ascension, this movement that gives us the feeling that beings mature and grow up. But they are human beings, so they waste away. They are not good: sometimes they are good, sometimes evil. They don't hesitate to act in all kinds of unclassifiable ways, and they are open to everything that, in the chilliness of our imaginations, would plunge a character outside a "noble" scene. The story of Moses' youth, for example, is astonishing. There is no one more ordinary than Moses; he is a man who experiences all manner of unexpected passions within himself, our Moses who, for centuries, has been the Moses of Michelangelo and not the Moses of the Bible. The Bible's Moses cuts himself while shaving. He is afraid, he is a liar. He does many a thing under the table before being Up There with the other Tables. This is what the oneiric world of the Bible makes apparent to us. The light that bathes the Bible has the same crude and shameless color as the light that reigns over the unconscious. We are those who later on transform, displace, and canonize the Bible, paint and sculpt it another way.

To begin with, Jacob leaves. We always find departure connected to decisive dreams: the bed is pushed aside. The nature of the dream in or from which we dream is important. We may have to leave our bed like a river overflowing its bed. Perhaps leaving the legitimate bed is a condition of the dream. Jacob leaves, after an incident in which he robs his older brother Esau of his birthright, by deceiving old blind Isaac with his mother's help. At which old Isaac sends Jacob away far from this country toward another branch of the family. He places him at a distance and, at the same time, sends him off to live his life as an ordinary man, one who gets married, and so on. . . . Night falls, Jacob is abroad.

> Jacob left Beer-sheba, and went toward Haran. And he came to a certain place, and stayed there that night, because the sun had set. Taking one of the stones of the place, he put it under his head and lay down in that place to sleep. And he dreamed that there was a ladder set up on the earth, and the top of it reached to heaven; and behold, the angels of God were ascending and descending on it![13]

In my own version, inscribed forever in my dream room, I always see the same thing: the ladder and the angels' movement of ascent and descent. I was especially delighted by this crowd of *descending* angels.

Let me now return to this. This is actually the portrait of the first dream of my life: it is figurative, for me it is a ladder with one step. The other steps would be invented by the people climbing up and down the ladder. You have probably guessed that it is the figure of Jacob's ladder. I was introduced to dreams by Jacob's ladder when I was small. This passage comes early in the Bible, in the book of Genesis. I always felt glad, when I later grew up out of the Garden, that this dream came early in the Bible, that the Bible started dreaming quickly; I appropriated this dream. It remained my own version, and I realized much later when I reread the book and checked and looked for the story, that I had dropped some of its elements I did not like. I only kept Jacob, the ladder, and the stone—one element had completely disappeared from my memory: God. Let me read the passage again:

> Jacob left Beer-sheba, and went toward Haran. And he came to a certain place, and stayed there that night, because the sun had set. Taking one of the stones of the place, he put it under his head and lay down in that place to sleep. And he dreamed that there was a ladder set up on the earth, and the top of it reached to heaven; and behold, the angels of God were ascending and descending on it![14]

I stopped there. For me it was everything. What I particularly enjoyed was the fact that the angels went up *and down*. Had I read a version about angels ascending to Heaven I would not have been interested. What interested me was their *climbing down*. But the story continues:

> And behold, the Lord stood above it and said, "I am the Lord, the God of Abraham your father and the God of Isaac; and the land on which you lie I will give to you and to your descendants; and your descendants shall be like the dust of the earth, and you shall spread abroad to the west and to the east and to the north and to the south; and by you and your descendants shall all the families of the earth bless themselves. Behold, I am with you and will keep you wherever you go, and will bring you back to this land; for I will not leave you until I have done that of which I have spoken to you." Then Jacob woke from his sleep and said, "Surely the Lord is in this place; and I did not know it." And he was afraid, and said, "How awesome is this place! This is none other than the house of God, and this is the gate of heaven." [15]

As I said, I had forgotten God. Rereading I liked the fact that God is in the dream. He is not outside the dream. He is inside the dream.

The Bible continues in such a way that you never really know whether God is inside or outside the dream. He is inside—so you might think that this is where it occurs: that God and Jacob awake afterward from sleep.

As I reread this dream I realized there is a sequel I always eliminate. I always stop my memory at the pure vision of the angels climbing up and down. This is my ladder, this toing and froing of messengers whose journey interests me most when it descends. *The dream scene* was always far more important to me than the scene of revelation. It is the first dream. In order for the ladder that enables us to pass from one place to another to be set up, we have to leave. Moreover, if we follow Jacob's path, it's through a system of permitted transgressions, since Isaac blessed Jacob well in spite of himself; yet this is the way we must go, leaving home behind. Go toward foreign lands, toward the foreigner in ourselves. Traveling in the unconscious, that inner foreign country, foreign home, country of lost countries.

For this, the bed must be pulled aside; we must descend by the ladder hidden under the legal bed and, breaking all ties and rules, with blows of the axe, pass over to the other side.

Thus, in the beginning, it has to do with leaving "home" by passing through "the door" in the depths of oneself.

This is what the young Virginia does with amazing violence in *O Lustro,* a vast premonitory book written by Clarice Lispector at the age of twenty, as if she had already lived for fifty years.

I don't like the name Virginia but it makes sense when you read the book, for you soon feel there must have been an echo of Virginia Woolf, a woman doomed to drown. The important thing is strangely—for I don't believe Clarice Lispector age twenty did things on purpose, she was totally in the realm of the unconscious—the book does deal with virginity.

It starts with Virginia as a very young girl.

> She looked at herself in the mirror. Her white and delicate face lost in darkness, her eyes open wide, her inexpressive lips . . . and suddenly she shouts: But I want to be bought, otherwise I will kill myself, she shouted and observed her own face panicking, because of that sentence; and proud of her eagerness, she burst into a false low laugh. Yes yes she needed a secret life in order to be able to exist. Next instant she was serious again, tired, her heart was beating in darkness, slowly and red. A new element that had been strange until now had penetrated her body. She now knew that she was good but that her goodness did not exclude her unkindness (or her evil). This sensation was rather ancient, she had discovered it several days ago. A new desire was stabbing her heart. The desire of being even freer, getting out of the limits of her own life. This sentence, this wordly sentence turned round and round in her body like a simple force.[16]

The book unravels inside a character's body. Of course it is inside and outside but everything that happens outside, all the small events of outside life, are immediately caught and turned into feelings and relations to the body.

Then the book brings us to the frontier of the forbidden and helps us to trespass it. It is about going beyond, about breaking through the known, the human, and advancing in the direction of the terrifying, of our own end . . . there where *the other* begins.

> Going out of the limits of her life she did not know what she was saying while looking at herself in the mirror in the friend's room. I could kill them all, she thought with a smile and a new freedom, staring childishly at her image. . . . Where had the idea come from?—since that morning spent in the cave, questions sprang easily. And at each instant, in which direction was she going? She advanced by learning things of which she had not even felt the beginning during her life. Where had the idea come from? From her body. And what if her body was her destiny?[17]

The mirror episode continues:

> I am here in the mirror, she shouted brutal and happy. But what could she do and what couldn't she do? No, no, she did not want to wait for the opportunity to kill. She had to kill. But if she killed, she wanted it to be in full freedom, without waiting. That would be it, going out of the limits of her life, she didn't know what she was thinking. Suddenly exhausted. . . . And like a door that shuts very quickly, she sank into sleep and instantly dreamt.
>
> She dreamt that her strength took her openly to the end of the world. . . . A cruel and living impulse pushed her, drove her, and she would have liked to die forever, if dying had given her one instant of pure pleasure. At that point of gravity which her body had reached, she could give her own heart to bite.[18]

You will have noticed that all the metaphors we found in Kafka's description of reading emerge here. We are approaching the point where the self bursts apart, the hour of cruelty. In a while we will kill, that is, we will show the ferocity hidden in us. Kill whom? Always the same creature, the figure of our impossible innocence:

> While walking she saw a dog and at the price of a huge effort to come out of close waters as if to come out of what no one can do, she decided to kill him while walking. Defenseless he was wagging his tail, she thought of killing him and the idea was quite cold, but she did not like the coldness of the idea. She beckoned the dog onto the bridge over the river and with her foot, without any hesitation, pushed him to his death in the water. She heard him cry, she saw him carried away by the current, she saw him die, and serenely she went on her way. Serenely she went on looking for something. And she saw a man a man a man. His large trousers were sticking in the wind, the legs, the meagre legs. He was a mulatto, the man, the man. And his hair, my god, his hair was going white. Trembling with disgust she approached him between air and space and stopped. He too stopped, his old eyes waiting. Nothing on Virginia's face could let him suppose one instant what she was expecting. She had to talk and did not know what to say. She said:
>
> Take me.[19]

It is a dream, *Virginia's* dream, the dream of a virgin. In dreams we unvirgin ourselves. Now comes the third period in this violent adventure called writing: now comes the time *to say the worst.*

"My" writers, "my" sisters, "my" guides, what do they have in common? They have all written by the axe's light. They have sought bliss in savage conflict and have found it.

The state of creation, Tsvetaeva tells us in *Art in the Light of Conscience:*

> a state of obsession . . . (and of) "possession." Someone, something gets into you, your hand is an executant, not of you, but of something. Who is it? What, through you, wants to exist.
>
> The state of creation is this dream state where suddenly, obeying an unknown need, you burn the house down, you push a friend off the top of the mountain.

> Did you do it? Of course you did. (You're the one sleeping, you're the one *dreaming*.) Your act, your very own act, done with complete freedom, an act by you—without your conscience—naturally.[20]

In saying this, Tsvetaeva rehabilitates, makes reappear in us the part that has to do with destruction, contradiction, violence: something stronger than us that deprives us of what is most precious (see the School of the Dead). Pushing a friend or enemy is equally a crime before the law, yet it is not the same thing. My authors, those I love, they who are capable of burning the house down, of pushing a friend off the mountain top, are incapable of acting this out. They are able to write the violent potential in themselves. I say "in themselves" because I am wary of misunderstandings. We are a long way from those assassins we see on television who are both excused and justified. These are almost always, no, are always men who grant themselves the right to kill. I don't consider we have the right to murder. I differentiate between the assassination carried out for the mass media and what our authors do: the revelation of something ineluctably threatened and threatening, which appears as soon as there is a relation with the other, something we must deal with, which is why, no matter what we do, we are always caught out. It is this inevitable and terrible situation of fault, of the lost opportunities for saving the other in order to save ourselves that those who have chosen real humanitarian service, for example, deal with. The authors who are important to me know the extent to which we must bear what is unbearable. It suffices for us to be involved in some family saga for us to already be either the beneficiary or victim—though it amounts to the same thing, since the positions are endlessly exchanged—of injustice. This is true of the smallest as well as the most important details in stories of inheritance, as it is in stories about bodies and illness. Illnesses are our wounds, our vengeance, our cries, our calls, our metaphors. The most beautiful and tragic example is that of Clarice and her mother, a tied and nonuntiable relation of birth and death between mother and daughter. It is enough for us to have a child, especially if the child is already an adult, for us to know the link with life and death, with the invisible and endless assassination, the mortal omission on both sides. It is enough to have parents to be the child: the assassin.

Dreams, Engendering, Creation

What do dreams teach us about written creation?

I will only speak about my experiences *as a woman*. A woman who writes is a woman who dreams about children. Our dream children are innumerable. The writing time, which is like reading time—there is latency, there is prewriting—is accompanied by a child state, what Tsvetaeva calls the "state of creation." The unconscious tells us a book is a scene of childbirth, delivery, abortion, breast-feeding. The whole chronicle of childbearing is in play within the unconscious during the writing period. We will bring forth into the light of night innumerable children. Sometimes the child is the size of a leaf and it crumbles to pieces. Sometimes it is just a small piece of paper you put on the bed that is suddenly lost. You do not know whether it is the child who faded or whether it is you who forgot the child. Sometimes it comes into the world six months old, bigger than you are, and of course it speaks better than Shakespeare. Sometimes it's a sticky little girl stuck to your leg, sometimes it's a terrible cocklike little boy running mad in a room on four cock legs. The worst is the scene when the child emerges and then disappears. These are all metaphors for the state of potential creation.

First Dream

He was a delightful, colored, tame, dark-rose little bird playing with me in bed. I don't know how but suddenly he was no longer there, much to my distress. We looked for him in vain; was he in the corner of the room? No. In the bed then? We shook the covers, the sheets. Suddenly, there he was. My friend picked him up: he was dead! —Dead? Died of what? —Died of death no doubt. —No hope? —Do you want to take him? After all there might be a little bit of this love, this joy still in him. I made up my mind to do it. How horrible! The creature was absolutely stiff, yes, it was death, the opposite of what he was. No, no, I put him down. We'll find another one, the dream said.

Second Dream: It was almost the end of the world

The forests had caught fire but I hadn't yet noticed. I was completely preoccupied with my little daughter, a child I had loved so much and had been so delighted with and proud of. And now time had past. She was ten months old. She was small and silent. I was carrying her. I had come to the sea region with her. I was only supposed to check into the hotel in the evening. I was occupied with the child and expecting so much. Suddenly, a fire of terror broke out in me. This child isn't normal, I said to myself. Has she ever shown a sign of life? Of course it was obvious. I cradle myself in happiness, and the miscarried child returns. Hadn't I already known some? Hadn't I already had some? I understood—it was in the family. My terror grew. In the distance I saw my son and his wife. If they knew! We have backward daughters. Delusions. A pain in the heart. Immense sorrow. I contemplated the grave and undecipherable child. When will you begin to speak? I asked sadly. "Whenever you want," she loudly and distinctly replied. She had known how to speak, and even to speak remarkably, for ages. I was beside myself with joy. At ten months! Such language! I had the most extraordinary daughter in the world! I adore her. "What do you want me to call you?" I asked her with passion. "Nane" she immediately replied. —Oh no, that isn't possible! I already have Anne, I can't call you Anne too. —I said. None, she said. —None? (It's written as None, I thought. Which plays on Nun . . .) Why not? Such an extraordinary and willful name. Without even thinking she had used an English word. This child was a genius. I felt joy and pride. I came out with it everywhere. My daughter who can speak at ten months said "whenever you want" to me. It was at this point, while progressing through the town toward the beaches with my triumph, that I noticed in the distance, not so far, the first red streaks of fire! What is it? Conflagration. It was already devouring the countryside, the nearby farms, the forests. It would soon be upon us. And no way out. With the child in my arms, I contemplated flight. But where to? The fire was already ablaze on all sides, we're in the middle: it's upon us. I had thought of the swimming pool. A feeble idea. Staying in the water beneath the fire? I'll try. I hurried. There were already a number of people who had had the same idea at the pool. At a table on the edge, Mrs. U was hurriedly writing a list of people to inform in case of accident. She was doing this in an orderly way. She was right. I too should leave at least a few written signs in case of death. I set about it: badly equipped, a piece of paper, I write down my child's name: None. If I die and they find her, they must know who she is. Then I tell myself that None will not be enough. I must set down whose daughter she is. I scribbled, slipped the paper into None's playsuit. I was in the road with None, everything was on fire. Suddenly I thought about my son, my son. Ah! That's when my heart caught fire. I am willing to die with my daughter, but not separated from my son. The idea that something could happen to him—to him, alone—separated from us, is intolerable to me. I ran through the streets, looking for my son, shaken by sobs as if he were already dead, sure that he was already dead. I mourned him to death. Wasn't he at the front at the start of the war? I had no news, no doubt he died over there without us, or was lost; we would have separate deaths. I sobbed so hard my ribs were breaking; I ran through the fire, having won everything and lost everything in the same hour.

Third dream

Hand painting or "a woman's writing"

It's spring cleaning, the flying start. We were battling with dirt and disorder in the numerous great rooms of the university. I myself was throwing away, throwing out; the floor is littered with old papers and debris, there aren't any dustbins, but the cleaners will come, I hope. . . .
Now I was in front of the old church chest, in the large hectic room. And even though this was a Catholic church, I decided to turn my hands to it. The

big iron doors. And now under my hands the color surges, surges! Painting surges! At the touch of my hands, a cosmic landscape suddenly springs up on the iron door on the left; planet flowers that have just blossomed under my hands. I was going very quickly. I stroked the iron surface or rather I ran my fingers over it and the iron replied; the colors spread out gayly. Would I be able to get to the end? Would I succeed in covering the whole metal plate? Star flowers blossomed under my palms, springing up in a flash on the iron surface. I'm going very fast, faster; with all my strength I was racing with the unknown force that was painting, passing through my palms, coming from the furthest depths of the iron; silently I posed the call, still another iron panel. That's it! The church chest was magnificent: a world. The planets were breathing. I was proud. I went toward the backroom. I was going to fetch my friend J., who was tidying up. I boasted: I announced that I had painted the chest, I insisted that J. come and see my great accomplishment. When she at last gives in, as she is coming what did I see? Not the star creation on the painted chest, but a classic painting, à la Braque, with one of those guitars that have painted hips in the center, an overpolished cliché. Did you do that? admired J. Yes, I lied. Stunned. Could someone have redone it? Covered it over? The miraculous painting? The living marvel springing from the depths of the iron to the wondering and surprised call of my hands: had someone covered this blossoming night with this dead painting? Who would have done it? I said: yes. Falsely and out of surprise attributing to myself the classic work of one of the men I saw bustling about here and there in the room. Moreover, as I approached the sink, I saw "the painter" in action. There he was, next to the sink, with his box of colors. He had just placed a large green spot, there, on the painting with his brush. Had I painted? "Painted"? What does that mean? No: I called forth with my hands. The iron and I had given rise. That had happened to two bodies unknown to one another. Outside however a storm was brewing, the trees were swaying, a column of dust was advancing. . . .[21]

What comes up when you start writing are all the scenes of impotence, terror, or vast power. The unconscious tells a tale of the supernatural possibility (it is always supernatural) of bringing a child to light, but the miracle in the dream is that you can have a child even when you cannot have a child. Even if you are too young or too old to have a child, even if you are eighty, you can still carry a child and give it birth and milk. And sometimes the milk is black.

In its representation of children the dream brings all sorts of children and all sorts of books. The children who arrive in dreams have all the elements of a book. We know nothing about the book: it is the dream and the child who teach us everything. These children are the dreaming woman's children yet at the same time they are strangers. It's equally interesting whether they are boys or girls; sometimes it's a fetus, sometimes a bird. . . .

The foreign child has another form. In Herman Broch's *The Death of Virgil* there is always a child coming and going, a companion, guide, and counterpart to the dying Virgil. This is perhaps an exteriorized equivalent of what a woman lives inwardly. Between the child (the text, that is) and the author, there is a relationship of absolute intensity, since it is a matter of life and death; we are constantly caught not ensuring life. If we don't hate castration, such a dream will make us abhor it. There is also a reversal in the maternal relation between child and mother, since life is exchanged.

While insisting on this primitive scene I should add that the fact the book is lived absolutely by the mother or author cannot but have effects on the writing. I am talking here about writers who dream. These stakes—will I or will I not give life?—will I succeed?—mixed with love and terror—cannot but echo in the text.

A woman's dreams are full of enjoyment, full of terror. I must say I am full of curiosity about men. I don't know how men dream when they start writing, though I do wonder about it. I can't imagine they dream that they bear children. So it must be something else. I'd like to know what the equivalent or substitute is.

Our books are dream children. They are ours, though they are total strangers. The sex is usually and strangely determined. The child appearing in the dream that is the text is always much stronger than we are. We don't know where they come from. The child adopts us, we obey, then we abandon the child, though in fact it is the child who abandons us. Everything is reversible. Even if we think we are writing the book, it is the book that is leading us. We depend entirely on the book's goodwill. This is what makes for the writer's humbleness and the fear and hope of seeing the book come to maturation.

Other types of dreams are common to men and women. You may dream of various types of transportation, all kinds of metaphors. But if you see a car coming you can be sure you are not going to drive it: you'll find yourself sitting in the back seat with the car racing like a horse, and all you can do is pray that it will not kill you. Perhaps you'll avoid the car accident, perhaps you'll avoid the miscarriage. I noted with surprise that in the early novel, *O Lustro,* as well as in Clarice Lispector's last novel, *The Hour of the Star,* which I spoke about earlier, the same stroke of fate recurred. In fact I first read *The Hour of the Star* ten years ago and I have only just read *O Lustro,* which is the younger of the two books. Both books end in the same brutal way—with a car accident and the character's death. It is as if they are imitating something connected to the life and death of a book. Writing is this, it is being played by life and death.

◧

Dreams Our Masters

Dreams teach us. They teach us how to write in four lessons:

Without Transition

A dream's charm is that you are transported into another world; no, you are not transported, you *are* already in the other world. The scene is that of the other world. There is no transition: you wake up in the dream in the other world, on the other side; there is no passport, no visa but this extreme familiarity with extreme strangeness. When you come as a foreigner to the United States it all takes so long—the passport, the visa, and so on—that you become accustomed to being foreign long before landing. It is a traumatic experience. In dreams you are spared this, the feeling of foreigness is absolutely pure, and this is the best thing for writing. Foreignness becomes a fantastic nationality.

Our dreams are the greatest poets. They are like Rimbaud's poems. The problem is that we usually destroy our dreams the moment we wake up, or everyone would be a poet. There is no formality, no introduction: you open the book and already you are a long way inside the country of writing.

Speed

This is how Jean Genet opens *The Thief's Journal:* "Le vêtement des forçats est rayé rose et blanc." [22] The moment we read this extraordinary first line we are instantly convicted. In English: "Convicts' garb is striped pink and white." [23]

> Si, commandé par mon coeur l'univers où je me complais, je l'élus, ai-je le pouvoir au moins d'y découvrir les nombreux sens que je veux: *Il existe donc un étroit rapport entre les fleurs et les bagnards.* [24]
>
> Though it was at my heart's bidding that I chose the universe wherein I delight, I at least have the power of finding therein the many meanings I wish to find: there is a close relationship between flowers and convicts. [25]

Either you reject the book or you are already striped pink and white. It is so immediate and powerful: it tells instantly of things we are not used to, the deepest secrets of a certain world. You know how novels are supposed to begin, with circumstances: In 18 . . . you might have seen a gentleman, etc., in the town of Nestles, etc., . . . This one begins with:

"Le vêtement des forçats"—that is the subject, the hero of this admirable book. In addition, "striped" comes in as something that will actually cross, stripe, cut the writing; the way will be "cut" right through the text. When you read in French: "Si, commandé par mon coeur l'univers où je me complais, je l'élus," you are immediately transported, without realizing it, not just to another world but also to another century; it is written in the layout, with the scansion and vocabulary of the great century of French writing. In addition, it plays instantly on the signifiers, so when we read: "je l'élus," (translated by "I chose" in English, which is unsatisfactory; it should be "I elected him"), in French we also hear something else, i.e., "I read it"—"je l'ai lu." This is typical dream writing.

Crossing the frontiers to the other world without transition, at the stroke of a signifier, this is what dreams permit us to do and why, if we are dreamers, we love dreams so much. It's the cancellation of opposition between inside and outside, there is no explanation: any explanation would destroy the magic. There is no suspense: the scene is immediately in the other world. Dreams are like "The Deserts of Love,"[26] they are poems. They grant us what we don't always have in life: speed. The passage is of lightening speed: there is no passage, no introduction, no entrance. This is perhaps what I like most in writing fiction, compared to the torment I feel when writing for the theater. There are enterings in the theater: you can't just fall out of the sky but must walk all the way—"an entrance" in the theater is the time needed for the other characters to join us on stage.

In the text, as in dreams, there is no entrance. I offer this as a test to all apprentice-writers: if you are marking time you are not yet there. In the text, as in the dream, you're right there. Moreover, this is why texts can create resistance in a certain number of readers. Many readers cannot stand to have the stranger right here. If you haven't, as a reader, burned your house down, if you are still at home, then you don't want to go abroad. People who don't like what I call "the text" are phobic, they are people who, in other situations, dislike being displaced.

The Taste of the Secret

This is how Clarice Lispector starts *O Lustro:*

> She would be fluid all her life, but what had accused her contours and had attracted the contours to a center, what had illuminated her against the world and had given it an intimate power, that had been the secret.[27]

This is the first sentence of this book. I like a book that begins like this. It begins inside, in the body.

These are books you can read. These are real books. You open the book and you have already crossed the border. You are in the text. You are in the world of the text. You are already in the other country. It already shines of the other country. We are already there by a multitude of signs. And yet we understand nothing. This is how we enter a book. We are blind and ignorant and gradually things become clearer. In Genet's text there is garb; the garb will be in play from beginning to end, like the convicts, like the eternal garb's stripe—all the more violent and magnificent since in this text (which he wrote before the destruction of the convict prisons) he mourns their passing.[28] Genet talks to us in the present tense about the eternal nature of the convict prisons. For all eternity the convicts' garb will be striped pink and white. Everything is instantly barred, striped, cut. . . .

The subject "The convicts' garb" enters.

"She would be fluid all her life." The subject "she" enters.

"She would be fluid all her life": the entire book is carried by this fluidity that we also find in *The Stream of Life*—which does not mean it is formless.[29] Clarice knows what fluidity is:

> But what had accused her contours and had attracted them toward a center, what had illuminated her against the world and had given it an intimate power, that had been the secret. Secret about which she would never be able to think in clear terms, for fear of invading and dissolving her image. And which yet had crystallized in the furthest

> depths of herself a remote and living seed and had never lost its magic—feeding her with its insoluble vagueness as the only reality that in her own eyes would always have to be lost.[30]

We immediately feel its power: it is instantly located at a level of reading that will later on oblige her to add a warning for the reader in *The Passion According to G. H.* Not everyone is interested in this type of secret. It is not the secret of the crime—which she is also capable of writing about—but this one:

> Standing on the fragile bridge, both were bending over the river and Virginia anxiously felt herself tremble unsteadily as if her naked feet were floating on the calm waves of the waters. It was a dry and violent day, composed of great flat tints; the trees were creaking in the warm wind contorted by sudden chills. Shivers of fresh air blew through her thin torn little-girl's dress. Her serious mouth pressed on the dead branch of the bridge, Virginia looked absent-mindedly into the water. Suddenly, she froze, tense and light:
>
> —Look!
>
> Daniel had rapidly turned his head—a drenched hat, caught on a rock, weltered down and darkened by the water was resisting the attempt of the river's flux to carry it off. Until it finally lost its strength, and, carried away by the rapid current, disappeared, tossing about in the foam bubbles almost as if it were happy. They hesitated in surprise.
>
> —We can't tell anyone, Virginia finally whispered in a distant and giddy voice.
>
> —Yes . . . even her brother had been frightened and he agreed . . . the waters continued their course—Even if they question us about the drown . . .
>
> —Yes! Virginia nearly screamed . . . they forced themselves to calm down, their eyes wild and wide-open.[31]

We are immediately in an extraordinary condensation of effects. From the first paragraph we are inside something that will go deep:

the meditation, a form of inner, indirect monologue, in the third person, pulls us toward an inaccessible center: "what accused her contours and attracted them toward a center." And without changing paragraphs suddenly we are "standing on the fragile bridge, both were bending over the river." The text says to us: fluid, secret, center, inside; then this interior secret that remains secret—since we don't know what it is—is suddenly increased twofold by the appearance of an exterior and visible secret, which is described to us: "Look!" The secret will be this hat, which isn't just anyone since it "was resisting. Until it finally lost its strength. . . ." It is preceded in the sentence by "Daniel had rapidly turned his head." The system of strength is fluid, it is transferred from one subject to another in the sentence. There is the objective materialization of a second secret: the first secret is from time immemorial and precedes the scene. The second secret is sealed immediately: "We can't tell anyone." We are in the world of secrets of all kinds. One calls up another, gives rise to another: so we don't know if we are inside or outside, or if we are one or two. She is two: "both were bending over the river and Virginia anxiously . . ."—"both" is obviously Virginia. Daniel comes later.

I hope this sounds mysterious to you. We are immediately drawn into the center where there is the secret. Do you want to know what the secret is? You can't because it is a secret.

> Secret about which she would never be able to think in clear terms . . . and which had yet crystallized in the furthest depths of herself to a remote and living seed that had never lost its magic feeding her in its insoluble vagueness as the only reality that in her own eyes would always have to be lost.

Can you imagine those lines written by a woman of twenty? It continues deeper inside the novel.

> Standing on the fragile bridge, both were bending over the river

Suddenly, a "both" has sprung up on the bridge/text. But the *both* remains unnamed, unknown, secret.

> and Virginia anxiously felt herself tremble unsteadily as if her naked feet were floating on the calm waves of the waters. It was a dry and violent day, composed of great flat tints; the trees were creaking in the warm wind contorted by sudden chills. Shivers of fresh air blew through her thin torn little-girl's dress. . . . Virginia looked absent-mindedly into the waters. Suddenly, she froze, tense and light:
>
> —Look!

And what do we see:

> a drenched hat, caught on a rock, weltered down and darkened by the water was resisting the attempt of the river's flux to carry it off.

The hat behaves exactly like a human being.

> Until it finally lost its strength, and, carried away by the rapid current, disappeared, tossing about in the foam bubbles almost as if it were happy. They hesitated in surprise.
>
> —We can't tell anyone, Virginia finally whispered in a distant and giddy voice.

The hat, we guess, is an *unheimlich* synecdoche for a drowned person, and "we can't tell anyone" is the second secret. But the general secret, the main secret life is made up of, we will never know.

It is the feeling of secret we become acquainted with when we dream, that is what makes us both enjoy and at the same time fear dreaming. When you are possessed by a dream, when you are the inhabitant of a dream, you are driven by this, by a kind of heart beating: and the dream says something that is never said, that will never be said by anyone else and which you unknow; you possess the unknown secret. It is this, not the possibility of knowing the secret, that makes you both dream and write: the beating presence of it, its feeling.

Clearly, dreams also bring us other things. One of them is the incredible situation Clarice Lispector dares to show. It is a form of exercise in sexuality that has nothing to do with perversity or eroticism but is the living illustration of those paradoxes, contradictions, and difficulties in our relation to the other. In the episode I started quoting, which went up to the meeting with the strange mulatto, you will have noticed the crudeness of the man's description. It starts with "a man a man a man" and Clarice Lispector has inscribed the almost racist connotation on purpose. She has not invented; probably she noted down one of her own dreams. It is not written to deal with racism, but to bring a person to the extremity of the acceptable, to the point where you start rejecting. (*The Passion According to G. H.* exhibits the same type of behavior: the woman consciously eats a cockroach, a *barata* [feminine in Brazilian], it is as if this woman were eating the archaic woman.)

> And like a door that closes quickly without slamming, she fell asleep at once. And dreamed instantly.
>
> She dreamt that her strength said very softly at the remotest ends of the world: I want to go beyond the limits of my life, wordlessly, with only obscure strength to guide me.[32]

I feel moved when I read that. It's already *The Passion According to G. H.* Today she is dreaming it; she will write it thirty years later.

> A cruel and living impulse pushed her, drove her, and she would have liked to die forever if dying had given her one instant of pure pleasure. At that point of gravity which her body had reached, she could give her own heart to bite. She wanted to go beyond the limits of her own life as a means of supreme cruelty. Then she went out of the house and left in search, searching with all the ferociousness she possessed: she was looking for an inspiration, her nostrils were sensitive like those of a delicate and frightened animal, but gentleness was all around her and she already knew gentleness, and henceforth gentleness would be the absence of fear and danger. She was going to do something that would go so far beyond the limits that she would never understand it—but she didn't have the necessary strength, ah! she couldn't go beyond what she could. She had to close her eyes for an instant and pray for herself with brutal con-

> tempt, until, with a deep sigh, ridding herself of the final pain, warmed up at last, she walked to the fateful sacrifice. Serenely she went on her way. Serenely she went on looking for something. And she saw a man, a man, a man. His large trousers were sticking in the wind, the legs, the meagre legs. He was a mulatto, the man, the man. And his hair, my God, his hair was going white. Trembling with disgust she approached him between air and space and stopped. He too stopped, his old eyes waiting. Nothing on Virginia's face could let him suppose one instant what she was expecting. She had to talk and did not know what to say. She said:
>
> —Take me.
>
> The mulatto's eyes opened wide, and at once cut out against the pure air and the wind, against the clear dark green of the grass and the trees, at once he began to laugh, he had understood. Silently, he picked her up, laughing, his whitening hair, laughing, and behind him the prairie spread out beneath the wind. Silently, he picked her up laughing, a wiff of chewed meat came from his mouth, from his stomach through his mouth, a breath of blood. Long dirty hairs stuck out of his open shirt and the air around him was lively, he picked her up by the arms and the ridiculous sensation hardened her with ferociousness—and he swung her in the air, proving to her she was light. She pushed him away violently and he silently, laughing, silently, began to walk and dragged her invincible and kissed her. But he was still laughing when she stood up again and serenely, as if at last going beyond the limits of her life, she calmly and forcibly trampled the man's wrinkled face, and spit upon him while he looked at her without understanding and the sky spread out into the uniformity of the blue sky. She woke up immediately and when she opened her eyes, she was almost standing, with a limpid and anxious face. Motionless, she felt her own body in its extremity, grown-up, with appeased and satisfied muscles.[33]

Virginia goes further than she can, further than she goes in reality: she is still very young and she does what is impossible. It is an experience in which Virginia (who is both the dreamer and the one who is dreamt, making it impossible for us to decide whether she has been raped or whether she rapes herself) loses what we call in French "her flower" (I need the word because of Genet and because of what I will tell you tomorrow). She is no longer a virgin—except as Virginia—since she knows everything about relations between men and women; it transforms her completely in her real life: though I don't know which is the real life except that the dream life is of course the most real. I know no example in writing of such a violent dream. One must be both a powerful dreamer and a powerful writer to transcribe it and give it to the public to read. She is author of her virginity and her rape—which is the result of what she calls her strength—thanks to the dream.

The dog came back in order to be killed. This is also remarkable, not because there has been a dog's murder, but because Clarice Lispector is so directly energized by the unconscious that when she was young she already knew—though not in a knowledgeable way—of all the mysteries that make for great writing and living.

Dreams remind us that there is a treasure locked away somewhere, and writing is the means to try and approach the treasure. And as we know, the treasure is in the searching, not the finding.

If I could, I would be jealous of dreams: they are mightier than we are, greater in weakness and in strength. In dreams we become magic, which is why if I could be jealous of my dreams—and I sometimes am—I would be.

The Dream Teaches Us "The Pure Element of Fear"

My authors are dreamers: they have understood what Tsvetaeva develops magnificently in "Pushkin and Pugachev": that the unconscious is at the source.[34] I am not speaking in Freudian terms: it has to do with the source of instincts that will be the motors of writing, what Tsvetaeva calls, when she tells the story of the "pathfinder," "the pure element of fear." As in the tales of Grimm and Perrault she suggests that it is the fear, the delight in fear, we enjoy, a delight we cannot enjoy in reality since we fear for our skin. Conversely, Tsvetaeva tells us, a fairy tale that doesn't frighten is not a fairy tale. It is terror that transports us to the place where Dostoyevsky was transported when he was condemned to death, this most precious place, the most alive, where you tell yourself you are going to receive the axe's blow, and where you discover, by the axe's light, what Kafka made Moses say: How beautiful the world is even in its ugliness. It's at this moment, as Blanchot would say, that "we see the light." It's at this moment, in extremis, that we are born and enjoy the strange things that can happen during such a dangerous, magnificent, and cruel experience as losing a relative while still in the freshness of childhood or youth. We feel, to our unspeakable horror, something that is extremely odd: on the one hand an infinitely greater loss than the one we feel when we are of a mature age, and on the other, an unavowable joy—difficult to perceive—that is simply the joy of being alive.

The pure joy of feeling that I am not the one who is dying. Proof of life: the feeling that there is death and life and that the axe did not fall on me. We feel this ephemeral, jubilatory joy following the loss of a loved one like a flash of lightening, then it's erased since it doesn't belong to human feeling. It is erased so that only those who have had the experience know it; the others have difficulty even imagining it. Age contributes to this, since we have a relation to mourning and loss that matures and changes with time.

The Lost Mysteries

Dreams remind us of mysteries. The mysteries we need are those that have been lost: these only resurface as something reopens. For a mother and daughter between whom there is an illness such as cancer—I say mother and daughter because it's the most intense relationship, the closest as far as the body is concerned—unheard-of things occur that can never exist in everyday life, which are yet the very secret of our lives. When I say cancer, I do so to evoke a threat that everyone knows, takes seriously, lives—a moment of the highest and strongest feelings of life. If we have lost everything in reality, dreams enable us to restore those moments when we are greatest, strongest in strength and in weakness—when we are *magic*.

The Magic Word

What we find in dreams is "the pure element of fear." When Tsvetaeva uses the word *element* it evokes something material, it is as if she were indicating the pure *substance*, something chemical, something concrete, that you find, fear, taste, perceive in dreams. In "Pushkin and Pugachev" she writes:

> There are magical words, magical apart from their meanings, [we are already in the "element"] physically magical, with a magic inherent in the sound itself, words that before they deliver a message already have a meaning, words that are signs and meanings unto themselves, that do not require comprehension, but only hearing, words of the animals, the child's dream language.
>
> It is possible that each person has in his own life his own magic words.
>
> In my life, the magic word was and remains—the Pathfinder.[35]

This is good news, because if you haven't yet found your own personal magic words, you still have time to find them. Everyone has their own magic words. The moment you find your magic word—it may be one word or it may be several—then you have the key, you can start writing.

For Genet, as Derrida has magically shown in his extraordinary book *Glas*, it was both the most and least obvious of words: his own name, *genêt*.

Tsvetaeva goes on to say:

> If they had asked me, a seven-year-old girl in a seven-fold sleep: "What is the name of the work where you meet Savelich and Lieu-

> tenant Grinev and the Empress Catherine the Second?" I would have answered right away: "The Pathfinder." Even now the whole *Captain's Daughter* is *that* word and has *that* name.[36]

The Pathfinder is that unknown thing that is, at the same time, the most known thing: that black spot in the distance amid the murky maelstrom of the blizzard toward which, as she says so beautifully, "poets will walk without thinking as if walking home." And she adds:

> Oh, I fell in love with pathfinder right away,from that moment of the dream when the self-styled father, that is, the black-bearded peasant, who turns up on the bed instead of Grinev's father, looked at me with laughing eyes. And when the peasant, grabbing the axe, started brandishing it right and left, I knew that I, that is, Grinev, that we would come out whole, and if I was afraid, it was the fear of dreams, and I luxuriated in the lack of suffering in the fear, in the possibility of going through the whole fear right to the very depths without suffering the consequences. (Thus, in a dream, you slow your pace on purpose, provoking the killer, knowing that at the last second, you'll fly away.) And when the frightening peasant started summoning me caressingly, saying: "Don't be afraid! Come here under the hand of my blessing!" I was already there under that blessing hand, standing there, and with all my considerable childish strength was pushing Grinev: "Well, go on then, go on, go on! Love him! Love him!" and I was ready to weep bitterly because Grinev *didn't* understand (Grinev isn't ever very strong on understanding) that the peasant loves him, the peasant lacks everyone, but loves him, the same as if a wolf suddenly were to give you a paw and you *didn't* take that paw.

The axe has returned. You can't come this way without meeting the axe and being enlightened by its light.

What about this scene with the axe and the peasant?

How glad I felt when I heard Tsvetaeva tell us with her frankness and habitual strength of this dream that founds her whole existence: it is not even—and this is the beautiful part—her own dream but a dream in one of Pushkin's books. What is marvelous is that the genealogy of writing is circumscribed in a system of stories about the mysteries of writing.

We might say that the poet Tsvetaeva has one of Pushkin's dreams for a grandfather. At the beginning of "My Pushkin," she tells us that she has come out of Pushkin's womb—womb from which is born her body, her vulnerability, and her strength. Then there is the dream in *The Captain's Daughter* told by little Grinev, which confirms and definitely inscribes this first intuition.

Grinev, the character who will dream, is a young sixteen-year-old aristocrat; the dream will take place in the fantastic storm:

> I was in that state of mind and feeling when reality gives way to dreams and merges into them in the shadowy visions of oncoming sleep. It seemed to me the storm was still raging and we were still wandering in the snowy desert. . . . Suddenly I saw a gateway and drove into the courtyard of our estate. My first thought was fear lest my father should be angry with me for my involuntary return and regard it as an intentional disobedience. Anxious, I jumped down from the chaise and saw my mother who came out to meet me on the steps, with an air of profound grief.
>
> 'Don't make any noise,' she said. 'Your father is ill; he is dying and wants to say good-bye to you.'
>
> Terror-stricken, I followed her to the bedroom. It was dimly lighted; people with sad-looking faces were standing by the bed. I approached the bed quietly; my mother lifted the bed-curtains and said: 'Andrey Petrovitch! Petrusha has come; he returned when he heard of your illness; bless him.' I knelt down and looked at the sick man. But what did I see? Instead of my father a black-bearded peasant lay on the bed looking at me merrily. I turned to my mother in perplexity, and said to her: 'What does it mean? This is not my father. And why should I ask this peasant's blessing?'—'Never mind, Petrusha,' my mother answered, 'he takes your father's place for the wedding; kiss his hand and he will bless you . . .' I would not do it.

> Then the peasant jumped off the bed, and seized an axe from behind his back, and began waving it about. I wanted to run away and could not; the room was full of dead bodies; I stumbled against them and slipped in the pools of blood. . . . The terrible peasant called to me kindly, saying: 'Don't be afraid, come and let me bless you.' Terror and confusion possessed me. . . . At that moment I woke up. The horses were standing; Savelyitch held me by the hand, saying:
>
> 'Come out, sir; we have arrived.' [37]

We have noticed the axe. We cannot even imagine how many axes there are in these stories. It's a primitive scene. Love and the axe are inseparable. Only the ones who love us can kill us. Those who love us kill us. And we kill those we love. This is what we cannot live. Only the dream tells us this.

I will add the speech Grinev made with Pushkin behind:

> I had a dream which I could never since forget and in which I still see a kind of prophecy when I reflect upon the strange vicissitudes of my life. The reader will forgive me, knowing from experience how natural it is for man to indulge in superstition, however great his contempt for all vain imaginings may be.

This is Grinev, the young sixteen-year-old who excuses himself, we might think, out of shyness. But this is not true: our authors know that the dream is not persona grata. This is moreover Freud's achievement: he defends the right to dream. Freud, however, is in his own home: he is emperor of his dreams.

Through Pushkin, Tsvetaeva tells us the secrets of love. She loves the peasant with the axe; she loves the one who crosses the line. Writing is situated at the turning point where Evil lets us see how it can be turned into Good and Good can be turned into Evil. She tells us we can enjoy all these axe blows, since we are in the dream's sacred space where all the rules that ordinarily make us excuse ourselves for the dream are waived. A space that is both totally free and totally limited. Genet says the same thing.

Remember the dream that closes *Miracle of the Rose.*[38] Genet writes long love stories in prison with a series of characters who all have one thing in common: they have been condemned to death—which is why Genet loves them.

We arrive at the end of the text:

> Someone opened Harcamone's door. He was sleeping on his back. First, four men entered his dream. Then he awoke. Without getting up, without even raising his torso, he turned his head to the door. He saw the black men and understood immediately, but he also realized very quickly that, in order to die in his sleep, he must not disrupt or destroy the state of dreaming in which he was still entangled. He decided to maintain the dream.[39]

I no longer know if the scene is in his dream or outside it, or whether he awakes in the dream. There are dreams in which we dream we are dreaming and dreams where we dream we are waking up. But here it is above all a structure of writing. In its indecision and power this writing originates totally from the dream.

> He therefore did not run his hand through his matted hair. He said "yes" to himself, and he felt a need to smile—but the smile was barely perceptible to the others—to smile inwardly so that the virtue of the smile would be transmitted to his inner being and he would be stronger than the moment, for the smile would ward off, despite his sadness, the tremendous gloom of his abandonment which threatened to drive him to despair, with all the pain it entails. He therefore smiled, with the faint smile he was to retain until his death. Above all, let it not be thought that he was intent on anything but the guillotine. His eyes were focused on it, but he decided to live ten heroic, that is, joyous, minutes. . . .Without growing an inch, he became huge, overtopping and splitting the cell, filling the universe, and the four black men shrank until they were no bigger than four bedbugs. The reader has realized that Harcamone was invested with such majesty that his clothes themselves were ennobled and turned to

silk and brocade. . . . Perhaps because of the miracle of which he was the place and object, or for some other reason—to give thanks to God his Father—he put his right knee on the floor. The four men quickly took advantage and climbed up his leg and sloping thigh. They had great difficulty, for the silk was slippery. Halfway up the thigh, forgoing his inaccessible and tumultous fly, they encountered his hand, which was lying in repose. They climbed on to it, and from there to the arm, and then to the lace sleeve. And finally to the right shoulder, the bowed neck, the left shoulder and, as lightly as possible, the face. Harcamone had not moved, except that he was breathing through his parted lips. The judge and the lawyer wormed their way into the ear and the chaplain and the executioner dared enter his mouth. They moved forward a little along the edge of the lower lip and fell into the gulf. And then, almost as soon as they passed the gullet, they came to a lane of trees that descended in a gentle, almost voluptous slope. All the foliage was very high and formed the sky of the landscape. They were unable to recognize the scents, for in states like theirs one can no longer distinguish particular features: one passes through forests, tramples down flowers, climbs over stones. What surprised them most was the silence. They nearly took each other by the hand, for in the interior of such a marvel the chaplain and the executioner became two lost schoolboys. They pressed onward, inspecting left and right, prospecting the silence, stumbling over moss, in order to get their bearings, but they found nothing. After a few hundred yards, it drew dark, though nothing had changed in that skyless landscape. They kicked around rather gaily the remains of a country fair: a spangled jersey, the ashes of a camp-fire, a circus-whip. Then, upon turning their heads, they realized that they had unwittingly been following a succession of winding paths more complicated than those of a mine. There was no end to Harcamone's interior. It was more decked with black than a capital whose king has just been assassinated. A voice from the heart declared: "The interior is grieving," and they swelled with fear, which rose within them like a light wind above the sea. They moved ahead, more lightly, between rocks and dizzying cliffs, some of them very close together, where no eagle flew. These walls kept converging. The men were approaching the inhuman regions of Harcamone.

. . . .

"The heart—have you found the heart?"

And realizing at once that none of them had found it, they continued their way along the corridor, tapping and listening to the mirrors. They advanced slowly, cupping their ears and often flattening them against the wall. It was the executioner who first heard the beats. They quickened their pace. They were now so frightened that they sped along the elastic ground in leaps and bounds of several yards. They were breathing hard and talking to themselves without a stop, as one does in dreams, that is, so softly and indistinctly that the words merely ruffle the silence. . . . Finally, the four dark men came to a mirror on which was drawn (obviously carved with the diamond of a ring) a heart pierced by an arrow. No doubt it was the portal of the heart. I don't know what gesture the executioner made, but it made the heart open and we entered the first chamber. It was bare, white and cold, without an aperture. . . . And that chamber was only the first. The mystery of the hidden chamber remained to be discovered. But no sooner did one of the four realize that they were not in the heart of the heart than a door opened by itself and we saw before us a red rose of monstrous size and beauty.

"The Mystic Rose," murmured the chaplain.

The four men were staggered by the splendour. The rays of the rose dazzled them at first, but they quickly pulled themselves together, for such people never permit themselves to show signs of respect. . . . Recovering from their agitation, they rushed in, pushing back the petals and crumpling them with their drunken hands, as a lecher who has been deprived of sex pushes back a whore's skirt. They were in the throes of drunken profanation. With their temples throbbing and their brows beaded with sweat, they reached the heart of the rose. It was a kind of dark well. At the very edge of this pit,

> which was as murky and deep as an eye, they leaned forward and were seized with a kind of dizziness. All four made the gestures of people losing their balance, and they toppled into the deep gaze.
>
> I heard the clopping of the horses that were bringing the wagon in which the victim was to be taken to the little cemetery.[40]

This is the dream of dreams in Genet's work. We have traveled through the succession of "rooms" and their equivalents (we could follow the same path in a great number of literary works, that is, the exploration of the greater by the smaller, from Rabelais to Swift). One scene is set upon another. The mystic scene and the erotic scene endlessly substitute for one another. Note that Genet cannot treat the extremely powerful ending to the text in any other way than by raising the dream ladder: only there does he have complete liberty; the scene shifts to what would be unspeakable elsewhere, the places of enunciation link up and succeed each other without discontinuity, to such an extent that we are the ones who fall through the famous hole.

As for Clarice's dreams, they are the authors of *The Stream of Life*. *The Stream of Life* is a night book. Yes, there *is* daylight, but to reach it she traverses the night. This night is not the nocturnal night. This Night is the universe of passage. From time to time, Clarice sleeps in order *to pass to the other side*. It's a voluntary act. "And I had decided that I was going to go to sleep so I could dream. I was yearning for the novelty of dreams."[41] Helped by the power of dreams, she is able to make her expeditions into the real. We must pass through dreams in order to perceive the supernatural dimension of the natural.

In *The Apple in the Dark* there is a passage that makes me think of Genet's scene, a passage, which also suddenly carries us away on the ladder, that comes right at the end of the text.[42] Genet's four characters are there: the chaplain, the executioner, the judge, and the lawyer who have ruled, governed, and mastered the individual's life in society. And there at the end is the truth. This is what Genet does. On the one hand he unveils his own fantasies to us, but from time to time he attacks other people's veils, lifting up the judges' and the lawyers' skirts, especially in his plays. In *Miracle of the Rose* he attacks the Law by saying that despite their fleshlessness, in the end the judges' only dream has been to sodomize the convict sentenced to death. The judges too desire to break down the interdicts, but they can only act it out in this terrible way.

Strangely enough, in *The Apple in the Dark,* Martin, who is assumed to have committed a crime—which he didn't really commit—is in the same position as Harcamone, and he tries to legitimate himself through the ridiculous puppet characters he is surrounded by. It doesn't work, and by the end of the text he truly reaches the other side.

◧

How Can We Finish a Book, a Dream?

What happens at the end of a text? Here again we have much to learn from what dreams, our masters, do with us; the author is in the book as we are in the dream's boat. We always have the belief and the illusion that we are the ones writing, that we are the ones dreaming. Clearly this isn't true. We are not having the dream, the dream has us, carries us, and, at a given moment, it drops us, even if the dream is in the author in the way the text is assumed to be. What we call texts escape us as the dream escapes us on waking, or the dream evades us in dreams. We follow it, things go at top speed, and we are constantly—what a giddy and delicious sensation!—surprised. In the dream as in the text, we go from one amazement to another. I imagine many texts are written completely differently, but I am only interested in the texts that escape. As an author I can say that if we are accidentally seized with worry about a text's ending then this is a totally peculiar experience, one that is disturbing and not necessarily agreeable. If we are completely lost we ask ourselves: How will this end? Will it end? And what if it doesn't end? This question can take hold of you. It's far more upsetting than the question of beginning. For one thing a text can have begun before us, which is the best way. For another, getting stuck with the beginning—an experience I have never had—is not so serious since we only have to wait. The text will end up by beginning. A text that presents itself but doesn't end questions the identity of what we are doing. But does a dream end? Perhaps we don't think about it much since it's a difficult moment. The fact that the end might escape us is perhaps the sensation we find most difficult to reconcile with. If the end escapes us where are we? A feeling similar to that of abandonment or the uprootedness we feel when we wake up badly looms. If the dream has stolen away we are inflicted with a more or less intense sensation of mourning. Books that don't want to end question the entire economy of our relationship to writing and to life. There are books that end all of a sudden. We were writing and suddenly it's over.

The example that comes to mind is one of Thomas Bernhard's books, which really made me laugh, although it isn't funny at all. This is how he writes, between the lines: inscribing the text's absolute liberty in relation to its masters and its population. The title of the text is *Alte Meister—Komödie*.[43] It performs in such a way that we are not aware of the hidden elements at stake in the text until we are kicked out of the text's door. The narrator is given an urgent appointment with an old friend in a museum. He is surprised since this is untypical of his old friend, who is an art critic. The text is extremely dense and compact, as Thomas Bernhard's texts are, though it turns upon itself since—contrary to *Ja,* where there is a narrative, where there is time—here there is neither narrative nor time.[44] We go to the appointment, we watch the time, there is inscription of spirals of remembrance concerning the relationship between the two friends, but everything is suspended on the initial enigma: how strange that he gave me an appointment in this place. What does he have to say to me? Why did he urge me to meet him today? The question recurs incessantly. And what are *we* doing? We're reading with one eye since we're waiting for the moment when the two friends will meet again. So, just as if we were waiting, we let ourselves get distracted, and absentmindedly read what is happening while waiting for the appointed time. Then we look at our watches and it's page 200. At last the meeting takes place. At a given moment, the old art critic says to the narrator: You must be wondering why I had you come today, at this hour? I will tell you but not right away. We're on page 220 in the museum room. Then the old critic asks the narrator if he wouldn't like to go to the theater with him that evening, because he has a seat. So the narrator says to himself: That's why he had me come! And *we* say: So we've read this entire book just to go to the theater! But what time is it? Then the other one says: Well, it's time to go, we must go quickly to the theater, they're playing "The Broken Jug" by Kleist. They hurry out. There are only two pages left. They hardly have time to see the play, which was a flop. And so it's over.

I adored this book. Genuine books are always like that: the site, the bed, the hope of another book. The whole time you were expecting to read the book, you were reading another book. The book in place of the book. What is the book written while you are preparing to write a book? There is no appointment with writing other than the one we go to wondering what we're doing here and where we're going. Meanwhile, our whole life passes through us and suddenly we're outside. Previously it wasn't the custom to write this kind of book. Writing the book obliquely. One didn't allow oneself to write the book that wasn't announced and let the space and time of the book be invaded by a totally unexpected book. A unique literary stroke of genius in this respect is Sterne's *Tristram Shandy*.

Writing giving in to itself: this is what happens in *O Lustro*. This book has neither beginning nor end. It is a place. It is what dreams teach us: not to be afraid of not being the driver, since it is frightening, when we write, to find ourselves riding a crazy book. The book writes itself, and if by chance the person opposite should ask you what you are writing, you have nothing to say since you don't know. Yet the book is written only if it has an engine. A book that writes itself and carries you on board must have an engine even if you don't know how it works, otherwise it will break down.

I Like Dream Writers

Tsvetaeva, Kafka, Clarice Lispector, Genet, Ingeborg Bachmann are all dreamers: sleepwalking scribes. I never really questioned the relationship to dreams of the authors I love. When I began to do this it turned out that they were all dreamers. What also transpired was just how much most books are outside dreams, how they avoid and resist dreams. It is surprising that there should be this refusal of such an important source. Wondering if "classical" writing hadn't prevented dreams, if there wasn't, in French literature for instance, a generalized distrust regarding dreamed productions, the only great dream I found going back through the centuries was Athaliah's well-known dream in Racine, a real dream around which everything is organized, rather as in *The Captain's Daughter*.

> Each of you lend me an attentive ear.
> I would not call to mind the past, nor would
> I give account unto you for the blood
> That I have shed . . .
>
> . . . A dream (why should a dream
> trouble me?) all my heart with fear imbues.
>
> . . . .
>
> . . . but then, forgetting care,
> His sweet charm and his noble, modest air
> I was admiring, suddenly I felt
> A murderous blade, which to the very hilt
> The traitor buried in my heart[45]

Everything is organized by the dream's power and something specifically tragic: an uncertainty; must we pay attention to the dream or not? There is a battle with the dream. Athaliah is a character of the unconscious, a rare character. She is surrounded by characters who belong, on the contrary, to the conscious scene. This discrepancy produces tragic effects. The contents of the dream are brutal: the dream stages the mother's death twice. There is something cyclical in the engendering of the matricide. The character's destiny is interesting when seen in perspective since it is a story about the putting to death. The second dream prophesies what will take place. I disliked *Athaliah*, because I once again found repetition of the ancient and formidable scene of the mother's assassination that has occurred from the beginning of time, although Athaliah herself appears to us as a bloodthirsty queen, as she says: "the blood that I have shed." It is a real dream however, a stroke of genius by Racine as Athaliah.

Elsewhere, there are few dreams, except in the world of the Romantics. I don't consider them as examples, but as exceptions—the French, the German, as well as the English Romantics. In literature there was a short "revolutionary" period, a breaking away—or return to—by the poet-children to the sources of genius: the Mother unconscious.

But what surprises me is the frequent distrust on the part of writers. I don't know where this is located, whether it precedes writing, whether authors are nondreamers, or whether perhaps for them repressing dreams is a condition for writing. Or is there a sense of reticence about starting from the unconscious in order to write? All this is however imaginary, since when we begin to write we are in a tradition, in an imaginary of that tradition, an imaginary of literature where we have in view imaginary laws we believe order the world of writing.

The History of My Dreams

I began to write in the regions of the unconscious. I had tremendous and clandestine relations with dreams; my dreams were so much stronger than I was I couldn't but obey them. But I had a disturbing sense of imposture. I kept thinking: what I have just written didn't come from me. *I* could write a thesis, but the texts I wrote were never mine. For a long time I lived in a state of serious uncertainty—sometimes I even told myself I shouldn't sign my name. Or else I felt great uneasiness when people talked to me about the texts "I" had written. They think it is me, but I only copy the other, it is dictated; and I don't know who the other is. In the same way that we don't govern our dreams, although I knew it was "the other" who arrived, I was never sure that "the other" would arrive. I had no memory of the history of my dreams. Had I always dreamed? And what if I didn't dream anymore? I was radically challenging the question of authority. It was perfectly justifiable naiveté. I detested the idea of calling myself an author or writer. It took twenty years before I could tolerate having this label attached to me as a definition.

What can we say if we are the stealers of dreams? Years later I ended up saying that we cannot think the experience: we must first of all respect the dream and that the formidable interdict against dreams is in relation to the general interdict and the fact that many of us, either permanently or temporarily, have lost the source. The occasional drying up of the dream is very frequent—it relates to what we can or cannot bear of our own regret. We have our desert periods. Putting oneself in relation to the unconscious is delicate, since we can't master the comings and goings, the gushings from the source. What I also learned is that the dream realms must not only be situated there where they exist primarily, under the bed, in the depths of the night, but that they must also exist in waking reality. It is terrible to think that you cannot write without the power of dreams. This power must be regained; we must therefore work to attain the same strength and intensity in reality as in dreams.

In this sense Clarice is exemplary. In "Love" the scene we have already referred to with the blindman is a dreamlike scene—it is a real scene, the text appears to be realist, but it has roots of meaning and revelation that go well beyond realism.[46] It plunges into the profoundest depths of our secrets; we could find the signifiers of this scene in a dream. These are the seemingly insignificant household signifiers that reveal and explode the walls that block our windows. Clarice has succeeded in bursting through the opaque screen that prevents us from seeing reality. This is what she talks about constantly in her texts—refinding in reality what we don't have the strength, the rapidity, the intelligence to perceive. An equivalent dream/reality is the scene Genet talks about in "What remained of a Rembrandt . . .": the short scene that takes place in a train carriage, a trifle starting from which everything is torn apart and the whole world tips over, just as it does in dreams.[47] It is difficult because you must literally rediscover the night hidden within the day, but it is not impossible: it is an exercise and must be done.

◧

Voyage to the Nearest Dreams

I don't go to just any strange Dreams. I go to those that resemble the ancient gardens where I spent a forgotten life, to those that spread out beneath the earth, before names, in the zones where music is spoken, where the languages before languages resound. I feel "at home" in Clarice Lispector's night.

> My vast night takes place in a primary state of latency. My hand rests upon the earth and listens hotly to the beating of a heart. I see the large white slug with a woman's breasts: is it a human entity? I burn it in an inquisitional fire. I possess the mysticism of the shadows of a remote past. And I leave these tortures of a victim with the indescribable mark that symbolizes life. Elementary creatures surround me, dwarfs, goblins, gnomes, and genies. I sacrifice animals to take from them the blood I need for my own occult ceremonies. In my fury I offer up the soul in its own blackness. The Mass terrifies me—I who perform it. And the turbid mind dominates all matter. The beast bares its teeth, and horses of allegorical chariots gallop through the distant air.
>
> In my night I idolize the secret meaning of the world. Mouth and tongue. And a loose horse, running free. I keep his hoof as a fetish. In the depths of my night there blows a crazed wind that brings me threads of cries.[48]

Cosmos night, where the winds of mysteries blow, those which, later on, when the era of writing comes, will take the form of odes and tragedies. I go, alive, there where I will go posthumously, to the times before time and the world beyond time. Over there I myself am no more than a dream.

Somewhere near a river I encounter Kafka's Dreams. We don't know one another though we recognize each other.

Kafka's dreams are of an extraordinary beauty, marvelously so since they are the *writing* of dreams. Here are two or three. One I have always loved is a trifle that says everything about Kafka's relationship to dreams:

> "Wrap your coat, O sublime dream, around the child."[49]

Kafka's dreams are angels without wings. Movements of the soul. Acts of goodness. Runnings. Infinitives. Verbs without subjects.

Here's another one:

> Who is it? Who walks under the trees of the quay? Who is quite lost? Who is past saving? Over whose grave does the grass grow? Dreams have arrived, upstream they came. They came, they climb up the wall of the quay on a ladder. One stops makes conversation with them, they know a number of things, but what they don't know is where they come from. It is quite warm this autumn evening. They turn toward the river and raise their arms. Why do you raise your arms instead of clasping us in them?"[50]

Here's another dream, with a title that makes us dream: "Inviolable Dream."

> She was running along the highroad. I didn't see her. I only noticed how she swung as she ran, how her veil flew, how her feet lifted; I was sitting at the edge of the field, gazing into the water in the little stream. She ran through the villages; children standing in the doorways watched her come and watched her go.[51]

If I cheated a little I could make a "montage" and tell you these are fragments from "The Deserts of Love."[52] It is exactly how Rimbaud writes: on board the dream. It so happens that Kafka did not work on this side: he wrote in a phantasmic rather than poetic way. His apprenticeship was as a guest of the dead, which is what enabled him to write an authorless dream. Nobody knows. Only the dream teaches us this sensation of "nobody knows"—in these short lines you feel all the emotions of "Les Déserts de l'amour," the race, the passage, the fearsome place of emotion—and yet it lies neither in the language, nor the grammar, nor the writing. I have always adored these unknown ones who walk along the quay. You can't write anything more magnificent than this loss which is the subject's severance, the nonrecognition that, far from remaining abstract, will be materialized to the point of the grass growing on the graves and, then, followed by the arrival of dreams.

These dreams: what we are when we are no longer ourselves: our survivings. Prophets of our traces, of our ultimate metamorphoses. Self-portraits of our future phantoms. Someone in us has a presentiment of future recognition. That will be me! we feel. Which is why we see them racing through the poets' nights.

Here they are again, appearing in Ingeborg Bachmann's astonished body. This is in *Night Flight:*

> Our field is the sky,
> tilled by the sweat of motors,
> in the face of night,
> at the risk of our dreams—
>
> . . . .
>
> Who lived there? Whose hands were pure?
> Who glowed in the night,
> a ghost to other ghosts?
>
> Who lives down below? Who cries . . .
> Who has lost the key to their house?
> Who can't find their bed, who is sleeping
> on the steps of the stairs? When morning comes, who will
> dare interpret the silvery trace: look above me. . . . When the

water pushes the watermill wheel once again,
who will dare remember the night?[53]

What Must We Do To Get to the School of Dreams?

This is the most urgent question. I know it is necessary to travel there. Do what Clarice does, for example: go to sleep: "And I had decided that I was going to go to sleep so I could dream. I was yearning for the novelty of dreams."[54]

Like plants, dreams have enemies, plant lice that devour them. The dream's enemy is interpretation. I used to read *The Interpretation of Dreams* with passion, but, though it is a marvelous book, it is a true dream-killer since it *interprets*. It wants to make the dream cough up. The dreams interpreted by Freud in *The Interpretation of Dreams* are all alike: although there is a difference in content, a different nucleus, the writing is the same. The dreams are written by Freud, both his own and those of other people. The flesh of the dream is no longer there. This is the great danger. We must know how to treat the dream as a dream, to leave it free, and to distrust all the exterior and interior demons that destroy dreams. We all have a demon, there is one hidden in the dream. This demon contrives to make the dream disappear the moment we move. We must let the dream transport us as Kafka lets his desire "to be a Red Indian" transport him.[55] We must let ourselves be carried on the dream's mane and must not wake up—something all dreamers know—while the dream is dictating the world to us. How can we do this? We must write at the dictation of our master the dream, a pencil in hand, straddling the mane at full gallop.

◧

There are few dreams in books. It's as if they have a bad reputation. There are fewer and fewer of them. Dreams used to occur in all the great books—in the Bible, in epic poems, in Greek literature, in the Babylonian epic poems, in Shakespeare—in an archaic mode, then they became more remote. I associate this increasing remoteness, this desiccation, with the diminishment of other signs. In the same way we find:

less and less poetry
less and less angels
less and less birds
less and less women
less and less courage.

Jacob wakes up, he gets up. What becomes of the ladder?

You have to take a rock, put it under your head, and let the dream ladder grow. It grows down—toward the depths.

The School of Roots

1. Birds, Women, and Writing

I am interested in a chain of associations and signifiers composed of birds, women, and writing. This may sound funny, it may sound gratuitous, but it is not. We only have to read the chapter in Leviticus in the Bible to realize that it is deadly serious. The chapter gives Moses and humanity in general laws on eating: dictating what is edible and what is not. In English the distinction is between meats that are *clean* and meats that are *unclean*. I need the French: in French *unclean* is *immonde,* which comes from the Latin *immundus;* it is the same word in Brazilian—*immundo*—and I'll need this later.

> And these are they which you shall have in abomination among the fowls, they shall not be eaten, they are an abomination, the eagle and the ossifrage and the vulture. And the owl and the nighthawk, and after his kind; and the little owl, and the great one; and the swan and the pelican, and the deer eagle. The stork, the heron and the lapling and the bat. All fowls that creep, going on all fours, shall be an abomination unto you.[1]

So this is what we are not supposed to eat. These are abominable. Why are they abominable? While there are others one can eat: for example:

> The locust and after his kind, and the bull locust after his kind. The beetle after his kind and the grasshopper after his kind. But all the creeping things which have four feet shall be an abomination unto you. And for these you shall be unclean.[2]

We can dream round the mystery of the stork's "immundity." We can have all kinds of reveries regarding the swan and the swan's abomination. And of course, if we were childlike enough, we'd worry; or, if we were Percival, we'd wonder why there are birds that are abominable. And we would have to accept the law's answer: Because. It is what the Bible says.

In *The Passion According to G. H.*, G. H., a woman reduced to her initials, encounters in complete solitude, face to face—even eye to eye—a cockroach, an abominable cockroach.[3] In Brazilian the word for cockroach is *barata,* and it is feminine. So a woman meets a barata, and it becomes the focus for a type of fantastic, total, emotional, spiritual, and intellectual revolution, which, in short, is a crime. The revolution leads G. H. to completely revise her clichéd way—our clichéd way—of thinking: our relations to the world in general and to living things in particular. She must deal with the phobia, with the horror we have of so-called abominable beings. I will now quote from a chapter in the middle of the book, after G. H. has had an initially ordinary reaction to the barata: that is, she has almost "killed" it by crushing it. A kind of white paste spurts out of the barata, which is nonetheless immortal. G. H. comes into contact with this paste; she starts thinking about what the white paste is and how to relate to it. This is what she says at one point:

> I had committed the forbidden act of touching something impure.[4]

In Brazilian "impure" is *immundo.*

> And so impure was I [so *immonde* was I], in my sudden indirect moment of self-knowledge, that I opened my mouth to call for help.[5]

The American translation continues:

> They proclaim, the Bible does, but if I understand what they proclaim, they will call me crazy. People like me had proclaimed that understanding them would be my destruction. "But you shall not eat the impure, the eagle, the griffon, and the hawk." Nor the owl, nor the swan, nor the bat, nor the stork, nor the entire tribe of crows.[6]

Now let me correct that translation. Actually G. H. does not say: "They proclaim, the Bible does . . ."

> E tao imunda estava eu, naquele meu subito conhecimento indirecto de mim, que abri a boca para pedir socorro. *Eles dizem tudo, a Biblia, eles dizem tudo*—mas se eu entender o que eles dizem, eles

> mesmos me chamarao de enlouquecida.[7] Pessoas iguais a mim haviam dito, no entanto entende-las seria a minha derrocada.
>
> "Mas nao comereis das impuras: quais sao a aguia, e o grifo, e o esmerilhao." E nem a coruja, e nem o cisne, e nem o morcego, nem a cegonha, e todo o gênero de corvos.[8]

What Clarice actually suggests is that the Bible is a masculine "they." One might have translated it like this: "Those He-Bible, those Bible, they say everything." It sounds awkward, but it is the way Clarice writes, awkwardly, roughly, and as truly as possible to what she wants us to feel.

So those He-Bible, it is *they* who tell us what is unclean and abominable. Clarice Lispector is a writer who has dealt throughout her work, among other questions, with this notion of the abominable in our lives, in all its forms. Let those birds be "abominable": I associate women and writing with this abomination. I do this, of course, half playfully, half seriously. It is my way of indicating the reserved, secluded, or excluded path or place where you meet those beings I think are worth knowing while we are alive. Those who belong to the birds and their kind (these may include some men), to writings and their kind: they are all to be found—and a fair company it is—outside; in a place that is called by Those Bible, those who are the Bible, abominable.

Elsewhere, outside, birds, women, and writing gather. *Not all* women however: quite a number of this kind linger inside, as we realize daily, and identify with "those-He-Bible" and their kind. Outside we shall find *all* those precious people who have not worried about respecting the law that separates what is and is not abominable according to Those Bible.

I have deliberately included Genet among those writers I have chosen to meet today. I wanted you to have the French version and the English translation, which is both correct and misleading. Genet is particularly difficult to translate: he inhabits a verbal land that resists all attempts at "naturalization" as we say in French. One has to travel to his elsewhere, that is meet him on his own idio-grounds and read along his specific paths in order to become acquainted with his universe.

This is like the writing of Clarice Lispector and those writers with whom I have a deep and everlasting love affair: Anna Akhmatova, Marina Tsvetaeva, Ingeborg Bachmann, Ossip Mandelstam. They all—without having decided to, without having met, without having read one another—inhabit what Genet calls in French: "les domaines inférieurs" (the nether realms).[9] They dwell somewhere in that most evasive of countries without a precise address, the one that is most difficult to find and work with, and where it is even difficult to live without effort, danger, risk. This risky country is situated somewhere near the unconscious: to reach it you have to go through the back door of thought.

If I gather these beings to talk about them in the same way, if I am worried by the fate of birds and women, it is because I have learned that not many people—unfortunately—or perhaps fortunately—can really love, tolerate, or understand a certain kind of writing; I am using women and birds as synonyms.

This is what Clarice Lispector wisely says at the beginning of *The Passion According to G. H.*[10] The translation says: "To potential readers." It should say: "To possible readers."

The translation says: "This is a book just like any other book" (106), so be reassured. But this is what Clarice Lispector says: "This book is like any other book."[11]

The translation goes on: "But I would be happy if it were read only by people whose outlook is fully formed."[12]

I don't know what "outlook" is, so let me tell you what Clarice says: "But I would be pleased if it were read only by persons whose souls are already mature."

And so I continue:

> Those who know that the approach to anything is done progressively and painfully—and includes as well passing through the opposite of what is being approached. These people and they alone will understand very slowly that this book takes nothing away from anyone. To me, for example, the character G. H. gradually gave a difficult joy; but it is called joy.[13]

This is how you are greeted when you open the book. You are told that this book is a book like others. Then you must ask yourself whether you are one of those persons whose souls are already mature. It is threatening, disquieting. Asking yourself: "Is my soul already mature" might sound prohibitive, but it isn't. The moment you read the next sentence you are either in or outside what is approaching. You must at least once in your life have realized you were undergoing the opposite of what was coming. I suppose this to be the case, but if it has not yet happened it will.

What comes next is most important: after having been severe Clarice says: "But this book does not take anything from anybody. To me, for example, the character G. H. gradually gave a difficult joy." In writing this Clarice Lispector wisely and emphatically sides with us readers: she is not the author, she is like us before the book. She too is reading it and has to deal with the character who comes to her in the book and gives her all kinds of emotions. Yet it is a warning that this book will give us pain, which is of course a joy. What about the book not *taking away* anything from anyone: the writing moves fast, and you might not even notice the remark, though I believe this to be one of the keys to our lives together. Each one of us—the whole of mankind, irrespective of sexual difference—must deal with the feeling of things being *taken away* from us. What is interesting is that birds, writing, and many women are considered abominable, threatening, and are *rejected,* because others, the rejectors, feel something is taken away from them. But let me leave women aside for today, since this is a controversial issue, and keep only birds and writing. Neither birds nor writing take anything away, yet people feel that some forms of writing do take something from us. Clarice Lispector has never been a feminist, Genet is not a feminist, though theirs are writings that may hurt, may dissatisfy, and give the feeling that something is taken away.

This is exactly (and I have chosen this example in order to make things clear) what happened to Gandhi. I imagine you believe he was for the most part adored; in fact he was hated and he is still hated today.

Hatred is still alive in India and he died of it. Those who were for Gandhi were mostly from what is called the scheduled castes, those who belong to the gutters with whom he had sided. Yet he did not ask anything of anyone; he simply went his own way. He did not ask people to change. He did what he felt he had to do. When people approached, he never asked, he never exacted anything from them, he never demanded anything from the people who approached him, not even his close friends: they went on living the way they wanted to live. But the simple fact that he lived according to his own law—which was ascetic and demanding of himself—was something that people could not tolerate. There are ways of writing that are perceived in the same way as Gandhi was perceived by the Indians.

Clarice Lispector had to deal with this perception, as did Ingeborg Bachmann and Tsvetaeva. Fortunately, there is always a small group who love such writings. But the majority are "those Bible."

Now what about what is called in French *l'immonde,* in Brazilian *imundo,* and in English *the unclean?* This is what Clarice says:

> I was knowing that the Bible's impure animals are forbidden because the imund is the root.[14] For there are things created that have never made themselves beautiful, and have stayed just as they were when created, and only they continue to be the entirely complete root, they are not to be eaten. The fruit of good and evil, the eating of living matter, would expel me from the paradise of adornment and require me to walk forever through the desert with a shepherd's staff. Many have been those who have walked in the desert with a staff.
>
> To build a possible soul, a soul whose head will not devour its own tail, the law commands that one uses only what is patently alive. And the law commands that whoever partakes of the imund, must do so without knowing; for, he who partakes of the imund knowing that it is imund, must also come to know that the imund is not imund. Is that it?[15]

She quotes the Bible:

> "And everything that crawls on the ground and has wings shall be imund, and shall not be eaten."
>
> I opened my mouth in fright to ask for help. Why? Because I did not want to become imund like the cockroach. What ideal held me from the sensing of an idea? Why should I not make myself imund? Exactly as I was revealing my whole self, what was I afraid of? Being imund? With what?
>
> Being imund with joy.[16]

That is my theme for today: to be "imund," to be unclean with joy. *Immonde,* that is, out of the *mundus* (the *world*). The monde, the world, that is so-called clean. The world that is on the good side of the law, that is "proper," the world of order. The moment you cross the line the law has drawn by wording, verb(aliz)ing, you are supposed to be out of the world. You no longer belong to the world.

Out there we shall be in the company of swans, storks, and griffons. Imagine this list on the other side, celebrated by someone like Dante. Dante loves birds, and in *Paradise* he has visions of birds like letters in the sky. So why are those birds imund? Because. As you know, this is the secret of the law: "because." This is the law's logic. It is this terrible "because," this senseless fatal "because" that has decided people's fate, even in the extremity of the concentration camps. People were divided, some were sent to gas chambers while others were "spared" for a later date, "because." It is this *because* that rules our lives. It pervades everything. It can even reach the fragile world of translation.

Now Clarice says explicitly that what is imund is joy. They are synonymous. Joy is imund, it is *not unclean:* if you use the English expression *unclean* you lose the necessary meaning "out of the world." Joy is out-of-the-world—this is what Clarice wants us to understand. It is true that what is really forbidden is enjoyment, jubilation. As Clarice says, with a stroke of genius, the point for Those Bible is that joy, jubilation, birds are forbidden because they are the root.

So the purpose of Those Bible is to forbid the root. This is what I wanted to bring to the surface, though we will not remain here; instead our ladder will grow down into the earth.

Writing is not put there, it does not happen out there, it does not come from outside. On the contrary, it comes from deep inside. It comes from what Genet calls the "nether realms," the inferior realms (*domaines inférieurs*). We'll try to go there for a time, since this is where the treasure of writing lies, where it is formed, where it has stayed since the beginning of creation: down below. The name of the place changes according to our writers. Some call it hell: it is of course a good, a desirable hell. This is what Clarice calls it: *inferno*. She does not always use the word hell but all kinds of parallel denominations ("*the other side*" cited in *The Stream of Life* is Tsvetaeva's abyss).[17] It is deep in my body, further down, behind thought. Thought comes in front of it and it closes like a door. This does not mean that it does not think, but it thinks differently from our thinking and speech. Somewhere in the depths of my heart, which is deeper than I think. Somewhere in my stomach, my womb, and if you have not got a womb—then it is somewhere "else." You must climb down in order to go in the direction of that place. But as I said yesterday, this sort of descent is much more difficult to achieve, much more tiring, much more physically exacting (*physically* because the soul is body), than climbing up. It is a climb, but it requires the whole strength of everything that is you—which I don't want to call "body," since it is more complex than the body—to go through the various doors, obstacles, walls, and distances we have forged to make a life. I know besides that what also prevents us in our society from going there is not our inability—because *all of us* are able—but our cowardice, our fear. Our fear, since we know perfectly well that we will reach the dangerous point where those who are excluded live—and we hate exclusion. This is our emotional, our personal, and political problem, the fact that we can't bear exclusion. We are afraid of it, we hate to be separated, that is why we are apt to commit all kinds of small crimes, self-denials, and treachery.

But one has to choose between losing what is mund and losing the best part of ourselves that is called imund. Since we are shaped by years and years of all kinds of experiences and education, we must travel through all sorts of places that are not necessarily pleasant to get there: our own marshes, our own mud. And yet it pays to do so. The trouble is we are not taught that it pays, that it is beneficial. We are not taught the pain nor that in pain is hidden joy. We don't know that we can fight against ourselves, against the accumulation of mental, emotional, and biographical clichés. The general trend in writing is a huge concatenation of clichés. It is a fight one must lead against subtle enemies. Our personal enemies in this fight are those Kafka denounced as preventing our return to paradise. Kafka insists paradise is not lost, it is there. But we are lazy and impatient. If we were neither lazy nor impatient we would be back in paradise. But we have to deal with this laziness and impatience. And of course with all the representatives of "Those Bible." There is a whole list of institutions, media, and machines that make for the banishment of birds, women. and writing. We are mistaken if we think *aparatchik* is a Russian word. Aparachtiks exist in all countries, especially in France; they are powerful against birds, i.e., women, i.e., writing, and people are afraid of them.

What is forbidden is unfortunately the best and that is joy. We are told by the law, "Thou shalt not eat of those birds, and thou shalt not read those books," i.e.: Thou shalt not eat of those books that are joy. Thomas Bernhard told us in "Montaigne" how when he was a child his family would say to him: if you go to the library and take a book you will go mad, insane; it is bad, wrong, rotten, vicious. Reading is a wonderful metaphor for all kinds of joy that are called vicious.

Tsvetaeva died early: she was a very strong, powerful, rebellious woman, much too powerful and full of joy to be allowed to survive. In a long poem called "The Poem of the End" there is a short line where she suddenly strikes out and says: "All poets are Yids." [18] The word is extremely insulting; it is a synonym of imund. Poets are unclean, abominable in the same way women are abominable. When Tsvetaeva used this word in the context of Russian society, the most abominable of the abominable at that time, poets, she felt, were *yids*. It was equivalent to all the other abominables. In another text she suggests that the abominable-she-loved, the abominable with whom she identified, was the nigger. So in the same line of substitutions you find: Jews, women, niggers, birds, poets, etc., all of them excluded and exiled. Exile is an uncomfortable situation, though it is also a magical situation. I am not making light of the experience of exile. But we can endure it differently. Some exiles die of rage, some transform their exile into a country. I understand those who die of (out)rage. It is what happened to Sakharov. Recently I met his wife, Elena Bonner, who is utterly mad with rage. She suffers day and night because all she feels is a desperate rage, which I do understand. Some exiles can draw joy from rage; those who are able to benefit from this strange experience relearn, recapture what we have lost. This was our experience as children, but we have lost the taste of bread, since, as Clarice Lispector says, we have eaten lobster in the meantime. We have lost the taste of hands, of the touching of hands. We have lost all the small and great secrets of joy. But the country of exile is not unattainable. It is even easier to go to that country, Exile, than it sometimes is to cross the border of a country like the United States.

2. The Passage of All Frontiers

A) Birth Certificates

We are going to a place to which the Christian imagination has given a negative connotation, that is, hell, but which, on the contrary, has a joyous (I don't want to say positive in opposition to the negative) connotation in the texts that are dear to me. Beginning by saying: we are going to hell, I am designating an approach I am perfectly aware I chose in a context I selected, and thereby privilege a certain place and path. Clearly, I am not the only one, for if I go in that direction it is because I am called by others, by those I love. Not everyone goes there. Preferring what some call hell to what some call paradise involves libidinal choices: for hell is paradise. I am not opposing them. I am simply working toward libidinal and geographical reorientation.

I have already pointed out that Genet called a certain place the "nether realms," which is obviously an equivalent. At the same time I notice that Genet speaks in terms of "realms" (*domaines*), in other words, he introduces the *dominus,* the master. He does this more or less consciously; I tend to think he does this rather more than less consciously, since Genet is someone who works on each word like a galley slave: in Genet's texts we are in the convict prison of language (although it's a good convict prison, since the convict prison is good for him). When Genet says "nether realms" (*domaines inférieurs*), I hear the master passing through.

Today we will work in a similar area, on the meeting between the economies of Genet and Clarice. Their economies are both similar and different, and I feel they are exemplary. Genet and Clarice are inhabitants of those countries that Genet deliberately and magnificently calls the "nether realms" and that Clarice calls not the "nether realms" but "hell." This is the word that appears in all her texts: in *The Stream of Life,* in *The Passion According to G. H.* There is not a single text by Clarice in which hell does not arise and arise jubilantly. Hell is a place of jouissance, a place of happiness; we might imagine that hell, despite its name, is situated celestially, though it is situated in the lower realms.

> And if many times I paint caves it's because they are my submersion into the earth, dark but clouded with charity, and I, nature's blood—extravagant and dangerous caves, Earth's talisman, where stalactites, fossils, and stones together and where creatures crazy through their own evil nature seek refuge. *Caves are my hell.*[19] Caves, dreamlike always with their mists, memory or longing? Frightening, frightening, esoteric, greenish with the ooze of time. Rats, with the crosslike wings of bats, hang glimmering in the dark cavern. I see black, hairy spiders. Rats and mice run frightened on the ground and along the walls. Among the stones the scorpion. Crabs, unchanged since prehistoric times, through countless births and deaths, would seem threatening beasts if they were human-sized. Ancient cockroaches drag themselves along in the half light. And all this am I. Everything is heavy with dreams when I paint a cave or write to you about one—out of it comes the clatter of dozens of unfettered horses to

> trample the shadows with dry hooves, and from the friction of the hooves the rejoicing liberates itself in sparks; here I am, the cave and I, in the time that will rot us.[20]

We will see this population, this swarming, this antiquity again in *The Passion According to G. H.* and in Genet. To get to the roots, that magic place, we must descend crossing over borders.

To *cross borders* is a cliché. A substantial, resourceful cliché. In *The Thief's Journal* Genet continually inscribes passing the frontiers (*le passage des frontières*), real crossing of the borders. There are real frontiers, from one country to the other, from France to Spain, Poland to Czechoslovakia, etc. To a French ear the expression rings like a cliché. But when Genet uses a cliché, which he does often, he does so deliberately. He strongly stresses the cliché to out-cliché the cliché, making the cliché cross the border it is.

In the following passage, concerned with the joy of hunger—a country of painful joy and wisdom mixed in the bread's dough—there is, as an example, a change of paragraph. We have been told a long story about a man called Stilitano, whom Genet is in love with, and the story closes with the sentence:

> "I went back to the hotel and told Stilitano about it. He said he would attend to the matter and left.
>
> I was born in Paris on December 19, 1910."[21]

This is how the text crosses the border. We are in the middle of the story with Stilitano, Stilitano leaves, exactly as if we were in the theater: "exit Stilitano. I was born in Paris. . . ." Stilitano left—I was born. The crossing of the border is so sudden and so subtle that we may not even realize we have crossed the border.

In Genet's scene of passing the border there is always an ambivalence, do we pass or don't we? Passing is subjected to all kinds of rites, either coded rites, such as passing through the army, or symbolic rites, the first of which is birth.

"I was born in Paris on December 19, 1910." Is this is an autobiography? On page 44 Genet is born; before he was not. As you can see, this happens long after birth. At the same time, it doesn't happen.

> "When I was twenty-one, I obtained a birth certificate." [22]

An accurate translation. Yet the French for certificate is the word *acte, Acte de naissance*. The paper itself, that is, the *form,* is called an *acte*. So it is at the age of twenty-one that Genet's Act of Birth is fulfilled. Now if you want to have an official paper or form filled out, you must have an *Acte de naissance* to exist. The French use the expression without realizing that it is such a rich word. For us it is just a piece of paper, an *acte de naissance*. So at twenty-one Genet tries to obtain an *acte de naissance,* that is, twenty-one years after his birth he looks for his birth act.

> My mother's name was Gabrielle Genet. My father remains unknown. I came into the world at 22 Rue d'Assas. [23]

We must take this literally.

> . . . 22 Rue d'Assas.
>
> "I'll find out something about my origin," I said to myself. . . . They refused to give me any information. I was brought up in Le Morvan by peasants. Whenever I meet broom [*genêt*] blossoms on the heaths—especially at twilight . . . I feel a deep sense of kinship with them. [24]

So that is how it happens. That is how we keep—without even realizing it—crossing invisible borders; we are at the Rue d'Assas, where they refuse to give us any information, but in the next sentence: "I was brought up in Le Morvan by peasants." It happens from sentence to sentence using every possible means, including the workings of time expressed in the changes of tense; the mother is past, the father remains present *as* the unknown, and so on. First Genet is twenty-one, then he is five.

The motor of this moment is the textual working on the passing of frontiers which in Genet, as in Clarice Lispector, plays on several registers. The familiar and uncanny (*unheimlich*) border passing would be the one we are all periodically subjected to—that from one country to another—but here it is metamorphosed into all crossings of all borders.

In *The Stream of Life* passing is the very definition of living:

> I'm very feverish . . . will I ever be able to stop living? Poor me, I die so much. I follow the tortuous path of roots breaking through the earth, for passion is my talent, in the burning of a dry tree I twist in the flames.[25]

Let's note: Clarice is following the root. We'll return to it.

All our primitive or poetic experiences are either separations or non-separations: the difficulty of defining the border between sexes, between species, and also between the high and the low.

Let's pass once again into Genet's country.

"I was born in Paris. . . ." That's the beginning, that's how autobiographies begin. But then *The Thief's Journal* begins with: "Convicts' garb is striped pink and white." *Je nais* later. There is phonetic play between *je nais* (I am born) and *Genet*. This is the theatrical setting up of everything connected with passing, with the frontier, birth, transition, descent, ancestry. He exits, he enters. "When I was twenty-one, I obtained a birth certificate." The birth certificate comes after birth, we never know when we pass the frontier, which direction we're going in; whether we are entering or exiting, or whether entering isn't exiting, etc. "My mother's name was Gabrielle Genet." There *is* origin, but the question is knowing whether this is or isn't origin, if it's the origin or not. The narrator is not absolutely sure about this. "My father remains unknown." Skidding through the tenses. There are a lot of numbers in the paragraph, there is the address, the date; we tell ourselves there is also origin, but in the end there is none.

> Number 22 was occupied by a Maternity Hospital. They refused to give me any information. I was brought up in Le Morvan by peasants. Whenever I meet broom [*genêt*] blossoms on the heaths.[26]

I was in the Rue d'Assas, here I am in Le Morvan, then on the heaths, by extremely rapid border crossings. This technique, this extraordinarily condensed writing, reminds us of the condensation and rapidity of dreams. Time falls out of step and indicates the crossing. It's a time that doesn't preserve our ordinary logic.

> Whenever I meet broom [*genêt*] blossoms on the heaths—especially at twilight on my way back from a visit to the ruins of Tiffauges where Gilles de Rais lived—I feel a deep sense of kinship with them. I regard them solemnly, with tenderness. My emotion seems ordained by all nature. I am alone in the world, and I am not sure that I am not the king—perhaps the sprite—of these flowers. They render homage as I pass, bow without bowing, but recognize me. They know that I am their living, moving, agile representative, conqueror of the wind. They are my natural emblem, but through them I have roots in that French soil which is fed by the powdered bones of the children and youths buggered, massacred, and burned by Gilles de Rais.[27]

Normally, I don't meet flowers, I meet people. We have slipped from one genre to another, one kingdom to another, one species to another.

If Genet writes "a deep sense of kinship with them," which is an intolerable cliché, it's because he is pulling us toward the depths. We are beginning to descend.

> I regard them solemnly, with tenderness. My emotion [*mon trouble*] seems ordained by all nature.[28]

The word *trouble* (translated into English by *emotion*) belongs to the Racinian domain; "all nature" comes from Rousseau's world.

> I am alone in the world . . .[29]

This is also Rousseau. Genet is playing with different stylistic periods, making us cross the stylistic border imperceptibly within the same paragraph.

> and I am not sure that I am not the king—perhaps the fairy—of these flowers.[31]

He lays down all his cards, but with the double negative we enter the world of rhetoric. We are going to put on gloves and high heels, we are going to speak elegantly. The king or the fairy? He or she? We don't know, we remain on the border, but the fairy counts more than the king.

> They render homage as I pass [we hear passage and man—*homme*—in *hommage*], bow without bowing [they bow physically but don't lower themselves], but recognize me.[31]

It's a fairy tale with recognition by flowers. Moreover the "but" doesn't indicate an opposition between "homage" and "recognize."

> They know that I am their living, moving, agile representative, conqueror of the wind.[32]

This is a fairy tale and he (Genet) is "naturally" in the flowers' place.

> They are my natural emblem, but through them I have roots.[33]

There is something childish in this "but."

> Through that thorny plant of the Cevennes, I take part in the criminal adventures of Vacher. Thus, through her whose name I bear, the vegetable kingdom is my familiar. I can regard all flowers without pity, they are members of my family. If, through them, I rejoin the nether realms—though it is to the bracken and their marshes, to the algae, that I should like to descend—I withdraw further from men.[34]

Now I am in a world under the world. The next paragraph begins with the planet Uranus, and through the stars the star world will also be inscribed. With this phallic thorn from the Cevennes I descend, and at the same time I come up. "Her whose name I bear" is Gabrielle Genet the mother, so there is a common link between the "thorny plant" and Gabrielle Genet. The mother, through a sexual sleight of hand, is not without "thorns." The vegetal world is my family. The name isn't here in this paragraph, it has been sewn into the text. "Gabrielle" is disseminated there, all her letters are present in *marécage* (marsh), *arb, elle*. She is there, cut up in pieces.

> I can regard all flowers without pity; they are members of my family. If, through them, I rejoin the nether realms—though it is to the bracken and their marshes, to the algae, that I should like to descend—I withdraw further from men.**[35]

It's true that if I descend into the "nether realms . . . I withdraw further from men," I am on the side of roots, or algae, or marshes, but at the same time I reach the nether realms of my desire, i.e., "men." I want to descend but I also want to ascend. Men are marked by this double star through which the text will climb back toward the sky.

> The atmosphere of the planet Uranus appears to be so heavy that the ferns there are creepers; the animals drag along, crushed by the weight of the gases.[36]

This is how Genet catches us: we are innocent, we believe we are following Clarice Lispector's root-wise path, and we find we have fallen flat on our backsides on the planet Ur/anus. It's a tremendous gag and yet at the same time there is an extremely serious side to it. The story recounts Genet's destiny, which is far from being insignificant. But then this she-man, who discovered the text's origin at the bottom of the ladder, goes from one line fragment to another, playing the text, twisting it, making fun of it, "pastiching" it, travestying it, endlessly making it travel.[37] He places language on the borderline of becoming a sexual object, exacting both jouissance and revenge.

Let's cross back over to Clarice Lispector's side. Here we arrive flat on our stomachs:

> Is it possible that without noticing it I've slipped over to the other side? The other side is a throbbingly infernal life. But there too is the transfiguration of my terror: I then deliver myself to a heavy life of heavy symbols, like ripe fruit. I choose the wrong similes, but they pull me along in their web. A minimal part of the memory of

my past's good sense still keeps me in touch with this side. Help me, because something is approaching and it's laughing at me. Quickly, save me!

But nobody can give me their hand so that I can escape: I have to use great strength—and in the nightmare I finally in a sudden convulsion fall prostrate back onto this side. I allow myself to remain splayed on the rough ground, exhausted, my heart stills beats wildly. I take in air in huge gulps. Am I safe? I wipe my wet brow. I stand up slowly, I try to take the first steps of a faltering recovery. I'm beginning to steady myself.

No, all this is not happening in real facts but rather in the domain of . . . of an art? Yes, of an artifice through which there arises a very delicate reality that comes to exist within me: that transfiguration has happened to me.

But the other side, from which I barely escaped, has become sacred, and to no one shall tell my secret.[38]

B) The Two Natures

THE WORD NATURE

When in *The Thief's Journal* I again cross the border, I don't know from which side I cross. Right at the entrance I see the word *nature* twinkling there, and naturally I pick, I pluck out the word. It's a natural word in Genet's work.

> Convicts' garb is striped pink and white . . . *there is a close relationship between flowers and convicts.* The fragility and delicacy of the former are of the same *nature* as the brutal insensitivity of the latter.
>
> The material evokes, both by its color and roughness, certain flowers whose petals are slightly fuzzy, which detail is sufficient for me to associate the idea of strength and shame with what is most *naturally* precious and fragile.[39]

The natural word, the word *nature,* has a sad fate: it was taken up in the great disputes, aimed in particular at people like myself who work on the sexual scene and who have been accused by a certain group of unenlightened people of using this word to mean a feminine or masculine nature—something I have never been able to conceive of—as if "nature" existed in opposition to "culture," or there were such a thing as pure nature. These disputes come from continents newly plunged in darkness. For a while, to flee the field of these sterile disputes, I no longer used the word *nature,* even though I adore it. Then I adopted it again. As soon as I use it in the domain of writing it begins to move, to twist a little, because in *writing* this is what it's all about. As soon as there is writing, it becomes a matter of *passage,* of all kinds of passages, of delimitation, of overflowing.

We cannot forget Ovid's *Metamorphoses.* There are metamorphoses of all kinds and genders here. Writing runs them through the other world, which is the world of writing. The primitive civilizations that preceded us, our mothers, believed in trance, in transformation, in transition, in transfer: one species passed into another, one realm became another, from the human to the mineral to the vegetal, in a generalized, infinite, magnificent, and unbounded way. By the word *nature* I don't necessarily mean the concept. I don't want to return here to philosophic thinking and the subject theme of crossing in its intersection and articulation with culture; I prefer to remain in the poetic space, which is also philosophical, naturally. When I say "I adopt again" I am rehabilitating, I am enjoying afresh the word *nature,* without being unaware that all kinds of adven*tures* happen to it in the text, including rhyme, and without being unaware of language clichés or on the contrary of great linguistic advances and impressions. As for language clichés I think of Bernhard who constantly says "natürlich" in his texts. It's a cliché that you find round the bend of every sentence in German.

Again, in Clarice's work we have a magnificent leitmotif that highlights nature. Here there is nature of all kinds. She designates nature as "supernature," as "supernatural." She stresses that there is nothing more supernatural than nature. We could change that and say: there is nothing more marvelous than the ordinary, but this is already more difficult to think. In Clarice Lispector's writing it is a question of rehabilitating what *is*. When I began to read Clarice I was enchanted by a tiny sentence in *The Stream of Life* that asked: "*And the turtles?*" [40] This is her oriflamme. The forgotten of the forgotten.

What would the two natures be for Clarice? The first, the one I love deeply, is the extraction from the repressed of what we are made of, i.e., *matter*. Clarice Lispector brings back more than the turtles to our feeble memories—because we notice tortoises from time to time; she returns the ability not to forget *matter*, which we don't notice: which we live, which we are. Clarice descends the ladder to the point of returning to think over matter. We are unable to think matter because we consider it to be invisible. We are made of assemblings that hide their truth, their atomic side, from us. We dislike matter, that is, ourselves, because we are destined to matter, because anonymous matter is called: death. Perhaps it isn't matter we dislike, perhaps it's *anonymity*. The anonymity to which we are destined—the loss of name—is what we repress at any price.

If we were what we no longer are, that is, small children, we would rediscover what Clarice has not lost: amazement before the *genetic* process. Am I playing with the word *genêt?* I have no idea. Perhaps I am. If it isn't me, it's my language's unconscious, which doesn't hesitate (ne se *gêne* pas) to enjoy linguistic atoms.

MY BORDERS

We are going to cross over borders, just as we recross borders, without knowing anything about it. Where is *our* border? When I cross a border, it's my border I'm crossing, though I don't know which one I'm crossing or which side I end up on. This is the charm of crossing the border. It is also what can constitute its distressing side.

The border makes up the homeland. It prohibits and gives passage in the same stroke.

The theme is explicit in *The Thief's Journal*, where it is repeated. Wherever border is indicated country is also indicated. Once again, we could go back ten thousand years, before the time of "country," and imagine the birth of borders. This is, however, unimaginable. Who invented the border? Borders don't exist. Borders are invisible lines that stir up war. They are as incredible as unicorns. Thus we might enter History, which is always a History of borders. Today we are in an era of the resurrection of nationalism. People are swollen with *home-neid* (home-envy). This home-neid is not only the need for a land and roof. It is primarily a need for the proper, for a proper country, for a proper name, a need for separation and, at the same time, a rejection of the other; it is less a need of difference than a distaste for difference, a desire to leave coupled with a desire to expel. A harsh, trenchant desire not to be you.

I want the word *dépays* (uncountry); I'm sorry we don't have it, since the *uncountry* is not supposed to exist. Only *pays* (country) and *dépaysement* exist. I like beings who belong to removal (*dépaysement*). People like Genet or Clarice are inhabitants of the uncountry, of the incountry, of the country hidden in the country, or lost in the country, of the other country, the country below, the country underneath.

How do we cross borders? It can be done in a completely indifferent and apathetic fashion, although the person who crosses borders in an indifferent fashion never crosses borders. The person who doesn't tremble while crossing a border doesn't know there is a border and doesn't cast doubt on their own definition. The person who trembles while crossing a border casts doubt on their own definition, not only on their passport, not only on their driver's license but also on every aspect and form of their definition; from the definition of age, which we talk about very little, to the definition that concerns us the whole time and which is, at the same time, the one we can't or won't reply to, that of sexual definition. What "nature" are we? What "species" are we?

WHAT KIND ARE WE? WHAT SEX ARE WE?

We have an easy relation with dogs. Are we dogs? Yes, according to Kafka. You may know Kafka's little animals who are bearers of his philosophy and his suffering. For example, in "Josephine the Singer or the Mouse Folk" Josephine's singing is so heart-gripping, so stunning, that all the mouse people swoon when they hear her sing.[41] But no one has ever heard Josephine sing because Josephine has no voice. In this magnificent short story everything is linked to the mystery of the voice. Sometimes a voice is a non-voice. This marvelous mouse is also terrifying because she is Kafka's last work, she is the Psyche of the dying Kafka, who had in effect lost his voice.

I remember reading in La Fontaine's *Fables* the metamorphosis of a mouse into a woman and a woman into a mouse.[42] I shivered because in our imaginary it isn't obvious that we desire or feel akin to mice. Maybe it's because we're afraid of being eaten by cats. We are, rather, dogs.

Dogs come to us from time to time, in Kafka's "A Dog's Searching," for example, as bearers of a special vision of the world.[43] They are us—us as dogs. *But what dog, what kind of dog are we?* This is what we ask in "A Dog's Searching." Once again, there is division: what species of dog am I? Lufthund? Air-dog? Earth-dog? We are transformed by animality. Texts of this kind should bring out our animal side. Perhaps the irony is that we are never more human than when we are dogs.

Perhaps there is an animal virtuality or potentiality dozing and awakening within us. In love relationships we have a tendency to give each other animal names. But we don't call each other vegetables as often. It is more difficult to elaborate upon our vegetable side and our identification with vegetables. If I have referred to these contiguities and overflowings, it is to emphasise that none of this can be done without the body.

Our body is the place of this questioning.

And what about the flower part in our body? I'm planting this question here and I'll let it grow.

C) The Author's Sext (C. L.)

One of the questions these frontier-runner texts ask us is: the question of sexual definition. *What is the author's sex?* It's an odd question. The author is a human being who writes, but writing is already a factor of change that is generally obstructed and repressed. Most writers don't like to see this question coming near them, but a few—and they are among the most important—allow the strangeness of this question to follow, stamp, and mark them. An author, in any case, has two worlds. Kafka expressed this by doing his portrait in two columns: on one side he put the household column and on the other the wild column, the column of writing; on one side the column in which he listed all the reasons to be a "proper" man, including everything that makes a man, a house, genitals, children, and on the other, everything that prevented him from being a "proper" man. With his habitual heartrending irony Kafka goes almost to the point of caricature, since he lived with the suffering of not managing to be the "proper" man his father imaged. The question is the same for Clarice, except that she didn't suffer from it at all, she never separated her life into two distinctly opposed columns, but constantly enjoyed the passage. "Naturally."

THE SEX OF A TEXT

Whenever I take an excerpt from *The Stream of Life* I always fail, I can't manage to cut it—it is always the page before instead of the page after that I would have liked to look at—for the simple reason that *The Stream of Life* is a single stream, a single current. And each time I make the idiotic move of taking a knife to cut water. This is the strength of this text. An easy trait to note when differentiating between economies is the trait of *lisible* "feminity" in a text by Clarice and that of *lisible* "masculinity" in a text by Genet. Cuts keep interfering in Genet's texts. Inside the pieces there is no cut since he has a double economy: while the text is clear-cut, inside there is a circuit of the order of "feminine" continuity. In Clarice's texts it is impossible to make a cut. The whole of her text is so necessary, she has descended so exactly to the place of writing that no matter where we are, we are always in the middle of writing.

In *The Stream of Life* we find all the atoms and elements of Genet's texts though reworked another way. The pass is different; the metamorphoses are there, we constantly pass from one realm to another, from one kind to another, at the same time and in the same trance, but, as Clarice says contrarily, in such a way that everything is naturalized.

> What does this improvised jazz bespeak? It bespeaks arms entangled in legs and flames rising and I passive like a piece of flesh that's devoured by the sharp hooked beak of an eagle that stops its blind flight. I express to myself and to you my most secret desires and with the words achieve a confused, orgiastic beauty. I shiver with pleasure in the midst of the innovation of using words that form intense underbrush! I struggle to conquer more freely the freedom that I have of sensations and thoughts without any utilatarian meaning: I'm alone, I and my freedom. My freedom is of such proportions that I could scandalize a savage, but I know you aren't scandalized with the plenitude that I achieve and that is without any perceptible frontiers. This capacity of mine to live what is round and full (ample)—I surround myself with carnivorous plants and legendary creatures (animals), all bathed in the coarse, awkward light of a mythical sex. I go ahead intuitively, and without looking for an idea: I'm organic. And I don't question myself about motives. I immerse myself in the near pain of an intense happiness (joy)—and to adorn me leaves and branches are born out of my hair.[44]

In this short passage, which is a tiny part of the immense space of *The Stream of Life,* you already have: arms, legs, flames, all of this is me—"flesh that's devoured by the sharp hooked beak of an eagle," "intense underbrush"—and so I have members, birds, underbrush, the round and the ample, a kind of geometry, carnivorous plants, animals, light, sex, etc. It's an endless Genet-like genesis.

I chose this passage, or rather this passage chose me, because of its mixed nature, arms and legs, and not only arms and legs but arms, legs, and flames, not only vision, but lost vision, blinded vision, for example lost blinded vision animated by what could have been a Promethean scene, except nothing is left but the sensation. Imagine Kafka's "Prometheus": it's marvelous, ten pages long and totally mad.[45] In Clarice it's "flesh that's devoured by the sharp hooked beak of an eagle," and this eagle is no trifle: it's interiorized. Everything that might have produced an image, a reference, or cliché is a world that doesn't exist. Only the sensation is left.

A tangling of arms, legs, kinds, and species as well as spheres, perspectives, and experiences: the one totally "organic," carnal, the other as if Clarice had invented another legendary, mythical realm or scene, in her own manner. For example, when she says "to adorn me leaves and branches are born out of my hair," this is both true and not true. The continuity, the contiguity, between the sensation and the fantasy is so perfect that it trances unceasingly, one is worth the other, one is lived as if it were the other.

I wanted to talk about *the sex of the author:* Clarice is right to say "mythical sex," though I don't know what "mythical" means. "All bathed in the coarse, awkward light of a mythical sex." There's the mystery. Why does this phrase enchant me, even though I can't give a logical account of it? I don't know what a "mythical sex" is, I don't know what the "light of a mythical sex" is, and even worse, I don't know why a "mythical sex" beams "coarse, awkward light." And all this enchants me. I could also be completely disenchanted and say that this doesn't mean anything. However I think the mystery is furtively stealing into us. We have capacities for living, as Clarice says, that are not defined as we normally define them. "This capacity of mine to live what is round and ample," for example, is not a current phrase. Eventually you get to the point where you say in an extremely elaborate way that you have the capacity to live something. I like the French expression: *avoir les doigts verts* (to have green fingers). That is already this type of crystallization. Having green fingers is having the capacity to give life to vegetation, and so, primitively, a continuity between fingers and vegetation is indicated in the language. It's somewhat the same thing here; we have either green or rainbow fingers, I don't know which. Clarice succeeds in noting that she has a capacity for what is "round and ample." Here she is also at the most primitive state of form and volume. It's as if she were capable of reading the signs of the body: not those of the unconscious, which is already speaking—the unconscious is a language—but the body signs that are of the same order as those of the unconscious, though before language.

The signs of the body: when you encounter someone who produces signs you can read the bodily signs of choices, angles, objects, positions. This is what Clarice notes: she is beneath thought, form, or codes, this is what she reads, what she deciphers—including her reading of herself. For example: "This capacity of mine to live what is round and ample—I surround myself with carnivorous plants and legendary animals." There's her self-portrait "all bathed," it is a cook's recipe: take that and that and soak it in "mythical sex" oil.

The "mythical sex" communicates something other beyond the nature of the nonmythical sex, something coarse and groping, as she says.

I note the word "legendary," I note the words "a mythical sex," and once again question the sex of the author who is brought to ask this question. The immersed author necessarily comes to the point of questioning his/her limits, his/her frontiers, his/her passages, his/her alterations: wondering not only which sex but also toward which sex, in which relation to the other, which other? What is the other's sex? This is not obvious: the author is not only the one who signs but also a completely unknown person blended with—and I'm keeping the word "legendary"—mythical, complex, variable consanguinity.

D) Genet's Frontier

Genet's frontier is a noon, a myth: the strangeness of the language, the skidding, twisting, crossing of borders is his very mark.

> La tapisserie intitulée "La Dame à la Licorne" m'a bouleversé pour des raisons que je n'entreprendrai pas ici d'énumérer. Mais, quand je passai, de Tchécoslovaquie en Pologne, la frontière, c'était un midi, l'été. La ligne idéale traversait un champs de seigle mûr, dont la blondeur était celle de la chevelure des jeunes Polonais; il avait la douceur un peu beurrée de la Pologne dont je savais qu'au cours de

l'histoire elle fut toujours blessée et plainte. J'étais avec un autre garçon expulsé comme moi par la police tchèque, mais je me perdis très vite, peut-être s'égara-t-il derrière un bosquet ou voulut-il m'abandonner: il disparut. Ce champ de seigle était bordé du côté polonais par un bois dont l'orée n'était que de bouleaux immobiles. Du côté tchèque d'un autre bois, mais de sapins. Longtemps je restai accroupi au bord, attentif à me demander ce que recélait ce champ, si je traversais quels douaniers invisibles les seigles dissimulaient. Des lièvres invisibles devaient le parcourir. J'étais inquiet. A midi, sous un ciel pur, la nature entière me proposait une énigme, et me la proposait avec suavité.

—S'il se produit quelque chose, me disais-je, c'est l'apparition d'une licorne. Un tel instant et un tel endroit ne peuvent accoucher qved'une licorne.

La peur, et la sorte d'émotion que j'éprouve toujours quand je passe une frontière, suscitaient à midi, sous un soleil de plomb la première féerie. Je me hasardai dans cette mer dorée comme on entre dans l'eau. Debout je traversai les seigles. Je m'avançai lentement, sûrement, avec la certitude d'être le personnage héraldique pour qui s'est formé le blason naturel: azur, champ d'or, soleil, forêts. Cette imagerie où je tenais ma place se compliquait de l'imagerie polonaise.

—"Dans ce ciel de midi doit planer, invisible, l'aigle blanc!"

En arrivant aux bouleaux, j'étais en Pologne. Un enchantement d'un autre ordre m'allait être proposé. La "Dame à la Licorne" m'est l'expression hautaine de ce passage de la ligne à midi. Je viens de connaître, grâce à la peur, un trouble en face du mystère de la nature diurne.[46]

The tapestry known as "Lady with the Unicorn" excited me for reasons which I shall not attempt to go into here. But when I crossed the border from Czechoslovakia into Poland, it was a summer afternoon [it was a noontime, in the summer].[47] The border ran through a field of ripe rye, the blondness of which was as blond as the hair of the young Poles; it had the somewhat buttery softness of Poland, about which I knew that in the course of history it was more

> sinned against than sinning. I was with another fellow who, like me, had been expelled by the Czech police, but I very soon lost sight of him; perhaps he had strayed off behind a bush or wanted to get rid of me. He disappeared. The rye field was bounded on the Polish side by a wood on whose edge was nothing but motionless birches; on the Czech side, by another wood, but of fir trees. I remained a long time squatting at the edge, intently wondering what lay hidden in the field. What if I crossed it? Were customs officers hidden in the rye? Invisible hares must have been running through it. I was uneasy. At noon, beneath a pure sky, all nature was offering me a puzzle, and offering it to me blandly.
>
> "If something happens," I said to myself, "it will be the appearance of a unicorn. Such a moment and such a place can only produce a unicorn."
>
> Fear, and the kind of emotion I always feel when I cross a border, conjured up at noon, beneath a leaden sun, the first fairyland. I ventured forth into that golden sea as one enters the water. I went through the rye standing up. I advanced slowly, surely, with the certainty of being the heraldic character for whom a natural blazon has been formed; azure, field of gold, sun, forests. This imagery, of which I was a part, was complicated by the Polish imagery.
>
> "In this noonday sky the white eagle should soar invisible!"
>
> When I got to the birches, I was in Poland. An enchantment of another order was about to be offered me. The "Lady with the Unicorn" is to me the lofty expression of this crossing the line at noontime. I had just experienced, as a result of fear, an uneasiness in the presence of the mystery of diurnal nature.[48]

"Mais, quand je passai, de Tchécoslovaquie en Pologne, la frontière, c'était un midi, l'été."

"*But* when I crossed the border from Czechoslovakia into Poland, it was a noontime, in the summer."[49]

We have already crossed over, yet here comes the border! We might also read: the border was a noontime. We are always either early or late as far as the construction of the passage is concerned. This "but" is a sort of simulacrum of an adversative clause. "But" signals a change in enunciation, as in an oral conversation. There are two registers of language: one level connotes the literary and uses all the elegant fittings of the French language, and this level is exchanged and mixed with the spoken level. But they are never separate. In the same way, there are sudden unexpected appearances of the historic past. There is also an inversion in the order of clauses, the border is rejected; subsequently it's on the other side, it circulates. Noon is the ideal line, the border in the day, as well as an endless noon/South (*midi*). The strange punctuation that mimes the border crossing breaks the classic style of the sentence. This is lost in translation.

The rhythm sings thus:

"La ligne idéale traversait un champ de seigle mûr, / dont la blondeur était celle de la chevelure / des jeunes Polonais; il avait la douceur / un peu beurrée de la Pologne / dont je savais qu'au cours de l'histoire / elle fut toujours blessée et plainte."

The border ran through a field of ripe rye, / the blondness of which was as blond as the hair / of young Poles; it had the somewhat buttery softness of Poland, / about which I knew that in the course of history / it was more sinned against than sinning.

These sentences have an aggravating rhythmic density since they tend toward the Alexandrine or classical verse. There is a simulation of poetic scansion that is not achieved. Unlike the choppy sentence that precedes it the sentence has no punctuation:

il avait la douceur un peu beurrée de la Pologne

it had the somewhat buttery softness of Poland

If we stay as close as possible to the enunciation we are in a kind of strangeness. But it's a sexual scene that steals in, with the help of the butter—"il avait la douceur un peu beurrée de la Pologne" / "it had the somewhat buttery softness of Poland"—and we hear the complaint (*la plainte*) and the wound (*la blessure*) of that scene. What puts us off the track is that everything is in the feminine gender in the French text, which is normal, since the buggered one is feminine.

There are other slippages at play on the phonetic level: *le beurrée* (the buttery) spreads through the whole text. It comes back in *l'orée* (the edge), in *dorée* (golden), shifting phonetically between butter and gold.

> La ligne idéale traversait un champs de seigle mûr, dont la blondeur était celle de la chevelure des jeunes Polonais; il avait la douceur un peu beurrée de la Pologne dont je savais qu'au cours de l'histoire elle fut toujours blessée et plainte. J'étais avec un autre garçon
>
> The border ran through a field of ripe rye, the blondness of which was as blond as the hair of young Poles; it had the somewhat buttery softness of Poland, about which I knew that in the course of history it was more sinned against than sinning [*more precisely*: *"it was always wounded and pitied"*]. I was with another fellow

The text shifts from the field to the fellow; there is substitution at work, to which we are preconsciously sensitive. We are impelled toward a type of humanization of this nature.

> J'étais avec un autre garçon expulsé comme moi par la police tchèque, mais je me perdis très vite, peut-être s'égara-t-il derrière un bosquet ou voulut-il m'abandonner: il disparut.
>
> I was with another fellow who, like me, had been expelled by the Czech police, but I very soon lost sight of him; perhaps he had strayed off behind a bush or wanted to get rid of me. He disappeared.

This fellow enters and exits. It is a rapid episode in relation to the longer episodes in *The Thief's Journal*. It is mimetic: we lose sight of the fellow since we are caught in this text that produces the effects of disappearance. We are astray, lost in the text, due to strange incidents like the one with this fellow and also because of the interesting amphibological function of the pronouns. None of the pronouns refers to a single subject, each time there is a double play, a twofold blow.

> Ce champ de seigle était bordé du côté polonais par un bois dont l'orée n'était que de bouleaux immobiles.

> The rye field was bounded on the Polish side by a wood at whose side was nothing but motionless birches.

Here again this way of twisting what is being said. *L'orée* (the edge) reinvokes *le beurrée* (the buttery), we keep hold of the sexual fantasy. *De bouleaux immobiles* (motionless birches) might play on motionless and anxiety, but it also plays on *de bout* (standing up): "Debout je traversai les seigles" / "I went through the rye standing up": and we will see *bouleau* (birch) again decomposed into *eau* (water). "Standing up" while he is "squatting." "Longtemps je restai accroupi au bord" / "I remained for a long time squatting on the edge." It is Proust who teaches us to begin a sentence with *longtemps* (for a long time). "Longtemps je me suis couché de bonne heure" / "For a long time I used to go to bed early." [50] The text now speaks Proustian.

> attentif à me demander ce que recélait ce champ, si je traversais quels douaniers les seigles dissimulaient

The tenses disagree. The sentence plays camouflaging a scene or time. This would not worry us if there wasn't "What if I crossed it?" which seems to command the presence or absence of the officers. As if that decision depended on *the decision* to cross. To cross through officers too.

> Longtemps je restai accroupi au bord, attentif à me demander ce que recélait ce champ, si je traversais quels douaniers invisibles les seigles dissimulaient.
>
> I remained a long time squatting at the edge, intently wondering what lay hidden in the field. What if I crossed customs officers hidden in the rye?

Everything is twisted. By the staging of the fantasy. "Des lièvres invisibles devaient le parcourir" / "Invisible hares must have been running through it"—we are made to think that the customs officers are hares: *quels douaniers*? (which customs officers?). Let's not forget that we are still in the famous tapestry where there are also hares besides the Unicorn and the Lady.

"I was uneasy" takes on an extraordinary importance in this linguistic space, suddenly it becomes such a simple phrase. It is like an oriflamme. In *The Thief's Journal* the leitmotif of uneasiness continues to flicker. Contrary to what we might imagine, if we are unaware of Genet's cunning, the uneasiness we dread is what he desires most, *uneasiness is the great figure of desire.* "I was uneasy" is almost an equivalent of "I was alive"; it's almost an equivalent of erection.

Here part of the tapestry enters:

> A midi, sous un ciel pur, la nature entière me proposait une énigme, et me la proposait avec suavité.
>
> At noon, beneath a pure sky, all nature was offering me a puzzle, and offering it to me blandly.

"Pure" is an emanation from "Lady with the Unicorn." We hear "all nature," nature is *en—tière* (a third party): to take one more step forward outside the cliché, nature is both whole and is there as a third party.

> S'il se produit quelque chose . . .
>
> If something happens . . .

It is none other than the appearance of a unicorn:

> c'est l'apparition d'une licorne
>
> it is the appearance of a unicorn

Again a twist in time, a present tense where we were expecting a future tense. All appearances are unicorns.

> Un tel instant et un tel endroit ne peuvent accoucher que d'une licorne.
>
> Such a moment and such a place can only produce a unicorn.

We enter the domain of labor, principal domain of Genet's fantasy. It plays on two registers, on the commonplace and the cliché.

> La peur, et la sorte d'émotion . . . suscitaient à midi, sous un soleil de plomb, la première féerie.

> Fear, and the kind of emotion . . . conjured up at noon, beneath a leaden sun, the first fairyhood.

This is the fairy's instigation. The "fairy" is "naturally" engendered by fear.

> Je me hasardai dans cette mer dorée comme on entre dans l'eau. Debout je traversais les seigles.
>
> I ventured forth into that golden sea as one enters the water. I went through the rye standing up.

We hear: I went through centuries (*siècles:* a close phonetic equivalent in French to *seigles,* that is, "rye"). The sea (*la mer*) divides between the mother (*la mère*) and water (*l'eau*) and the play on *bouleau* (birch) reappears. We are not traversing a fellow, we are traversing the sea (*la mer*). If we stay with Genet's cunning we see that this is the passage through the mother by the father-son or by the son-father, the engendering scene in which Genet is both the son and the father, and from which "the heraldic character" will suddenly arise.

> Je m'avançais lentement, sûrement, avec la certitude d'être le personnage héraldique . . .
>
> I advanced slowly, surely, with the certainty of being the heraldic character . . .

Earlier he had insisted he did not know who he was; here, on the contrary, he is both sure and certain. He is indeed the unicorn: it is not a little boy who is born, she is a feminine unicorn (*une licorne*—in French "unicorn" is of the feminine gender).

> Cette imagerie où je tenais ma place . . .
>
> This imagery, of which I was a part [where I had my place] . . .[51]

As a unicorn I at least have my place, whereas I don't have my place elsewhere. This becomes confused with the Polish imagery, which is homosexual. I was born according to a natural and heraldic process, with a supplementary touch figured in the Polish imagery.

Let's go back to the beginning of the paragraph:

> La tapisserie de "La Dame à la Licorne" m'a bouleversé pour des raisons que je n'entreprendrai pas ici d'énumérer.
>
> The tapestry known as "Lady with the Unicorn" excited me for reasons which I shall not attempt to go into here.

What had remained obscure in this sentence becomes clear through the development of this magnificent imagery. We discover why this tapestry excites him. He who couldn't find a trace of his birth when he went to 22 Rue d'Assas, finds it in the tapestry of the "Lady with the Unicorn." At the same time there is this touch of humor: but I won't tell you—and this "but" mocks the reader.

The appearance of the "white eagle" operates doubly: it is on the Polish coat of arms and in mythology, and as a mythological character it reminds us of many young men.

> Un enchantement d'un autre ordre m'allait être proposé.
>
> An enchantment of another order was about to be offered me.

The displacement of "me" in French, *m'allait être* instead of *allait m'être,* is not grammatically incorrect, it is simply disagreeable to the ear. We can hear *m'allaitait* (was nursing me), *mal-être* (discomfort), and also *mal* (bad). An enchantment of another order.

> La "Dame à la Licorne" me l'est l'expression hautaine . . .
>
> The 'Lady with the Unicorn' is to me the lofty expression . . .

We hear "La 'Dame à la Licorne' *mêle* l'expression hautaine. . . ." (*Mêler* in French is "to mix" or "to put in," *mêler son mot:* "to put in one's word.") "The 'Lady with the Unicorn' puts in lofty expression."

The vital question of birth, of giving birth, of this "natural" relationship, as Genet says, often in a humoristic manner, brings us to vegetal nature. We only have to follow the traces of border-nature, entering and exiting, to see what is at work in these metamorphoses and these feints.

3. The Word *Racine:* A Story of Proper Names

The word *racine* (root) has taken on a somewhat vulgar tint nowadays, rubbed in ideologies that have racist connotations. We must reduce it to ashes and wait for its rebirth. Then we will hear a very beautiful word. I thank Jean Racine, I return to my *racines* with Racine. The signifiers of our great writers work on us; the common proper name, the proper common name affects us, as readers, and especially the one whose name it is. We must all deal with the unconscious effects of our proper name. We find this aspect of language's intervention in our destiny on the flesh of our imagination. We work on writers whose names are bearers of textual effects. That doesn't mean I am attracted by authors whose names are at work in the language but simply that there aren't any names which don't produce such effects. This includes names that are seemingly insignificant, such as mine for example, an impossible name, but which has always produced signifying effects. Genet constantly puts his name to work in the French language. Entire works were born from his name. There is *corneille* (crow) in Corneille's texts: the bird, the relation to elevation, to flying, to a certain type of bird. If we take up Leviticus again, we will find all kinds of crows. Racine must translate the effects of roots (*racine*) in all his texts, especially the roots (*racines*) of the heart. In other words, I am only referring to the root (*racines*); since the proper name belongs to the order of roots, it is the lightest and most intangible root we have. It roots us, in language and beyond, without our knowing precisely where. One author whose name was not without signifying effects—of which he was perfectly well aware—is Kafka. In German, *Kafka* means *chouca* = *corneille* (crow). He too is a bird. He knows it, plays with it, inscribes it. In *Wedding Preparations in the Country and Other Posthumous Writings* and in the *Diaries* there are several instances of this type of small aphorisms that works on crows.[52] It's magnificent. The crows maintain that they can destroy the sky.

> The crows maintain that a single crow could destroy the heavens. There is no doubt about that, but it proves nothing against the heavens, for heaven simply means: the impossibility of crows.[53]

It's possible or it's impossible, no one can go and verify. Perhaps that's what going to the root is, going toward the unverifiable. As for Clarice Lispector's name, who could invent a name more promising of light or vision?

Here is a moment when Genet tells of his love for Salvador. Salvador is frightful.

> J'avais réussi à aimer le corps malingre, le visage gris, la barbe rare et ridiculement plantée. Salvador prenait soin de moi, mais la nuit, à la bougie, je recherchais dans les coutures de son pantalon les poux, nos familiers. Les poux nous habitaient.[54]

> I had managed to love that sickly body, gray face, and ridiculously sparse beard. Salvador took care of me, but at night, by candlelight, I hunted for lice, our pets, in the seams of his trousers. The lice inhabited us.[55]

Lice, our pets. The spouse inhabited us. Lice: Genet's spouse. (The French text plays on a phonetic equivalent *les poux* [lice] and *l'époux* [spouse].)

> A nos vêtements ils donnaient une animation, une présence qui, disparues, font qu'ils sont morts.

> Il était bien que je fusse l'amant du plus pauvre et du plus laid au fond de tant de misères. Pour cela je connus un état privilégié. J'eus du mal, mais chaque victoire obtenue—mes mains crasseuses orgueilleusement exposées m'aidaient à exposer orgueilleusement ma barbe et mes cheveux longs—me donnaient de la force—ou de la faiblesse, et c'est ici la même chose—pour la victoire suivante qui dans votre langage prendrait naturellement le nom de déchéance.[56]

> They imparted to our clothes an animation, a presence, which, when they had gone, left our garments lifeless.
>
> It was good that, in the depths of such wretchedness, I was the lover of the poorest and homeliest. I thereby had a rare privilege. I had difficulty, but every victory I achieved—my filthy hands, proudly exposed, helped me proudly expose my beard and long hair—gave me strength—or weakness, and here it amounts to the same thing—for the following victory, which in your language would naturally be called a comedown.[57]

Descent, comedown. By way of beggars we have just passed into the cultivation of sores. For Genet the descent is a movement ordered by the desire to heighten, to bring back up, to raise the lowest to a higher level.

> Ce m'aura été une très utile discipline, et qui me permet de tendrement sourire encore au plus humble parmi les détritus, qu'ils soient humains ou matériels, et jusqu'aux vomissures jusqu'à la salive que je laisse baver sur le visage de ma mère, jusqu'à vos excréments. Je conserverai en moi-même l'idée de moi-même mendiant.
>
> Je me voulais semblable à cette femme qui, à l'abri des gens, chez elle conserva sa fille, une sorte de monstre hideux, difforme, grognant et marchant a quatre pattes stupide et blanc. En accouchant son désespoir fut tel sans doute qu'il devint l'essence même de sa vie. Elle décida d'aimer ce monstre, d'aimer la laideur sortie de son ventre où elle s'était élaborée et de l'ériger dévotieusement. C'est en elle-même qu'elle ordonna un reposoir où elle conservait l'idée du monstre. Avec des soins dévôts, des mains douces malgré le cal des besognes quotidiennes, avec l'acharnement volontaire des désespérés elle s'opposa au monde, au monde elle opposa le monstre qui prit les proportions du monde et sa puissance. C'est à partir de lui que s'ordonnèrent de nouveaux principes, sans cesse combattus par les forces du monde qui venaient se heurter à elle mais s'arrêtaient au mur de sa demeure où sa fille était enfermée.
>
> (1) Par les journaux j'appris qu'après quarante ans de dévoue-

ment cette mère arrosa d'essence—ou de pétrole—sa fille endormie et mit le feu. Le monstre (la fille) succomba, des flammes on retira la vieille (75 ans), et elle fut sauvée, c'est-à-dire qu'elle comparut en cours d'assises.[58]

It proved to have been a very useful discipline for me and still enables me to smile tenderly at the humblest among the dregs, whether human or material, including vomit, including the saliva I let drool on my mother's face, including your excrement. I shall preserve within me the idea of myself as beggar.

I wanted to be like that woman who, at home, hidden away from people, sheltered her daughter, a kind of hideous, misshapen monster, stupid and white, who grunted and walked on all fours. When the mother gave birth, her despair was probably such that it became the very essence of her life. She decided to love this monster, to love the ugliness that had come out of her belly in which it had been elaborated, and to erect it devotedly. Within herself she ordained an altar where she preserved the idea of Monster. With devoted care, with hands gentle despite the calluses of her daily toil, with the willful zeal of the hopeless, she set herself up against the world, and against the world she set up the monster, which took on the proportions of the world and its power. It was on the basis of the monster that new principals were ordained, principles constantly combated by the forces of the world which came charging into her but which stopped at the walls of her dwelling where her daughter was confined.

(1) I learned from the newspapers that, after forty years of devotion, this mother sprayed her sleeping daughter, and then the whole house, with gasoline—or petroleum—and set fire to the house. The monster (the daughter) died. The old woman (age seventy-five) was rescued from the flames and was saved, that is, she was brought to trial.[59]

Here is the ultimate stage of the comedown which is at the same time the acme, the culminating point of the lowest and the highest.

> Je me voulus semblable à cette femme qui à l'abri des gens chez elle conserva sa fille une sorte de monstre.
>
> I wanted to be like that woman who, at home, hidden away from people, sheltered her daughter, a kind of hideous, misshapen monster.

His desire is to be a *woman* who, hidden away from people, keeps her daughter in herself, a kind of monster. This is his self-portrait: a woman who keeps an interiorized monster who is greater and more powerful than the world. The mother only comes in at the end, in the note, when she is condemned. In the note, in journalistic style, there is the monster/daughter, though it could be the mother, and further on the last metamorphosis, "the old woman (age seventy-five)."

Who is the monster? What is a monster?

With Clarice the descent to life is equally fierce and truculent. In *The Stream of Life* the descent leads Clarice to transform herself into someone violent: she is metamorphosed into a tiger.

> Us . . . facing the scandal of death.
>
> Listen only superficially to what I say and from the lack of meaning will be born a meaning, as from me light, ethereal life is inexplicably born. The dense jungle of words wraps itself thickly around what I feel and live, and transforms everything I am into something of my own that remains beyond me. Nature is all-encompassing; it coils around me and is sexually alive, just that and nothing more; just alive. I too am savagely alive—and I lick my snout like the tiger after it has devoured the deer.[60]

There's the resemblance, there's the difference.

CLARICE AND GENET: LIBIDINAL POSITIONS

Genet constantly puts a process of reversal into effect. He is absolutely clear on this subject. He exalts what is abased by society, what is considered inferior. Dregs are what he most esteems, what he likes most. His process is one of provocative contrast. He will praise the dirtiest being to the skies, and won't love a guy who doesn't have a louse on his neck. This process of reverse relief is, as he always insists, at once moving, magnificent, and magnifying. At the same time it is disquieting, since it undoes, undermines, and saps a social hierarchy, though this is in order to replace it with another hierarchy that is libidinal and imaginary.

For Clarice the strong opposition between the high and the low is not in play. If she descends it's because she desires to go to a place she describes in the passage from *The Stream of Life* as well as in hundreds of others. Clarice strains toward the beginning and end, toward what she develops throughout her work with variations as *matter*. Matter for her is not abstract but intelligent, alive, and powerful. One has to follow a path to arrive at matter, which has stages that are the natural grades of different realms and species. Clarice effects an interior return journey, since we began as matter before moving away from whence we came. She makes a return journey to our concrete origins, though the journey is a spiritual one. *The journey is spiritual* because it is not enough to put one's foot on the ground to come back to earth. It is an extremely difficult spiritual exercise, reintegrating the earthly, the earth, and the earth's composition in one's body, imagination, thought. Clarice does not do this simply: she proceeds by feeling her way, by desiring; she moves blindly, since she is an explorer in the domain, methodically, making mistakes. Sometimes she opens the wrong door, makes the wrong maneuvre; sometimes she gets very close to matter, to earth—she's almost there—then she takes a step too many and breaks through the earth, passes to the other side, and comes back on the side of abstraction and the idealizing thought she constantly criticizes. Realizing this, she returns once again, though unlike Genet there is no provocation in this process. For Genet, everything is defiance. There is no defiance in Clarice except of herself, she only attacks one enemy: the distortion and remoteness that are in her as they are in every human being. She does not have to act as if she is wounded as Genet does, nor does she have to exalt and seek the ignoble. She would find seeking the ignoble ignoble. But she is not in

Genet's case. She is not who Genet is. Whatever his inclination for mutation, change, and travestying, he is a man. Clarice is marked, she marks herself, feels, as a woman. We have here two examples of the affirmation of a type of sexual identity that produces ethical effects. So that when Clarice does something that seems to us to entail effort or violence and that we may feel as excessive, she actually does it without excessiveness and *without exaltation*.

4. Everything Ends with Flowers

Hell returns us to something mysterious and enchanted that we know nothing about but that is deep inside us: our genesis.

There are analogous stages in the journey toward the origin, in the return to roots, to what we learned in natural sciences about the constitution of the world. There is passage through the animal state, then through the vegetal state, and so we move away from humankind; from the vegetal we descend into the earth, by the stem, by the root, until we reach what doesn't concern us, although it exists and inscribes itself, which is of the mineral order, although it doesn't hold together since we are aiming toward disassembly, toward decomposition. Perhaps flowers are our last human stage. In the texts and biographies of Kafka, Genet, and Clarice Lispector, everything ends with flowers. In my opinion it is not an accident.

Kafka's last thoughts were for flowers. It's all the more remarkable because there are not many flowers in his texts. As he was dying he lost the ability to speak, since tuberculosis had affected his larynx he could not even drink. At this moment of extinction he put down what he had to say on small scraps of paper. They have been kept and are magnificent. I hope you have read these remnants of Kafka's works that are published under the title "Conversation Slips."[61] I loved Kafka because of these scraps of paper: they belong to the economy of the dying, yet in this economy, rapidity, and condensation there is something extraordinarily tender and precise. We might think it's telegraphic since he is exhausted, but although there is a shortage of personal pronouns poetry and delicacy are there.

> Somewhere in today's newspapers there is an excellent item on the treatment of cut flowers; they are so terribly thirsty, one more such newspaper.
>
> Sideways, that was almost my idea so they could drink more. Spread out the leaves.
>
> I'd like to take care of the peonies because they are so fragile.
>
> Move the lilacs into the sun.
>
> Do you have a moment, please? [You see, he was polite even on those slips of paper.] Then please spray the peonies.[62]

This is the most beautiful thing in the world. First, his concern, though the discourse itself is magnificent. It's the extraordinary courtesy of a man who has nothing left to live. The other exists.

> In this condition I am in, recuperating from it, if it is possible at all, will take me weeks. Please look and see that the peonies don't touch the bottom of the vase. This is why they have to be kept in bowls.[63]

A day later:

> See the lilacs? Fresh as the morning.[64]

And next to that you have:

> Can't the pains stop from time to time, I mean for a certain time?[65]

Or this sentence, which resumes Kafka's ironic energy, his old Jew side, and which always makes me laugh:

> Let the bad remain bad. Otherwise it will grow worse.

> But for the moment, there are enough flowers.
>
> Show me the gladiolus, it's too thin to be with the others.
>
> The red thorn is too hidden, too much in the shade.
>
> More water. Fruit.
>
> Last night still another bee drank the white lilac.
>
> Cut very much on the bias, that way they can touch the bottom.
>
> We can't find any cytisus?[66]

And one of the last sentences:

> How wonderful that is, isn't it? The lilac dying. It drinks, goes on swilling. It cannot be that a dying man drinks.[67]

And the last one:

> So the help goes away again, without helping.[68]

I remember being startled when I discovered that, strangely enough, Clarice had died with flowers. In the same circumstances. She too wrote on scraps of paper. These scraps were gathered up by her friend. There is a "style" of dying in which we find something economical, extremely dense, compact, urgent, and, at the same time, very tender.

Clarice wrote this on a slip of paper, since she could no longer speak, on December 9, 1977; I believe she died on the 9th or the 10th:

> A sudden lack of air. Long before the metamorphosis of my ill-being, I had already noticed in one of the paintings in my house a beginning.
>
> Me, me, if memory does not fail me, I shall die.[69]

We understand what she subtly means: if memory does not fail her, she will be alive when she dies. She will remember, she will know.

> I am a cherished object of God. And this is what gave birth to flowers in my bosom. He created me equal to what I am writing now: "I am a cherished object of God" and he liked having created me as I liked creating the sentence. And the more the human object has spirit the more God is satisfied.
>
> White lilies pressed against the nudity of my bosom. I offer white lilies to what hurts me in you. For we are beings who lack. This because certain things—if they are not given—wilt. For example, the lilies' petals would burn against the warmth of my body. I call the light breeze for my future death. I will have to die, otherwise my petals will burn. This is why I give myself up to death every day. I die and I am born again.
>
> Moreover, I have already died from the death of others. But now I am dying from drunkenness of life. And I bless the warmth of the living body that wilts white lilies.[70]

It sounds awkward, though not because I was improvising the translation but because she wrote that way. She did not care. She was writing according to what was happening, following what flowers dictated to her.

It is striking that these heroes of writing should come to the flower stage at the moment of dying. These flowers are not signs of death, they are alive. In these moments of extremity, perhaps we do admit to having a relationship with the vegetal, which is as intense, as embodied, as fleshly. I should not speak of it in the way I do, for I am not dying. It is only a guess. Perhaps it is because we discover at this point that flowers lead—in the way Genet said playfully, though he struck upon something true—by their way of getting through the earth, with their roots, to the core of the matter. They lead where we are going: we need them as guides. They are so fragile, as both Genet and Clarice say. They lead us back to the origins, where we become obviously one family.

The beauty of this text is exceptional. Clarice never wrote anything like this in her texts to be published, in which she constantly strives to rationalize, deepen, unfold another mystery. Whereas here, since she isn't concerned with reading, she is in a writing place without concession or compromise. We have recognized the traits, the ways of thinking, the allusions to what she calls "the metamorphosis" as well as to something of the order of what she calls "the Beginning," since dying is a beginning, it is something else beginning, something that was before and that begins again.

> He created me equal to what I am writing now: "I am the cherished object of God" and he liked having created me as I liked creating the sentence.

I am a sentence of God: this is a transposition. She is transposed. You cannot transpose. Even though she is always so attentive to grammar she remains in the place she has designated, she remains in the masculine: "he liked having created me" (*ele gostou de me ter criado*), she remains the object of God. She is truly in metamorphosis. She could have made the agreement and said *me ter criada*, but she is already an object. She is in transition toward something that is neither masculine nor feminine.

Here are flowers, which are inside and not inside. Inside or perhaps only inside. First we are told: "what gave birth to flowers in my bosom," then: "white lilies pressed against the nudity of my bosom." It is an interior nudity; we are in a generalized space of being inside. The whole relationship to flowers is both natural and simple, then more complicated to imagine: it is not realistic but a complex continuity that already makes for her passing from feminine to masculine, from subject to object, in this movement toward what we call death. I am sorry that in French we don't have the past historic of the verb *to die:* you cannot actively have your death in French, whereas in other languages you are given the freedom to die actively.

5. Toward the Book Without an Author

Do we have to be dying to go to the School of Roots? I do not know whether I should say yes or no. *No,* if it is taken literally and means that tomorrow we won't belong to this world anymore. Although this is something one should hope for. *Yes,* if we understand it to be an exercise in that delicate and respectful form of life we call dying. It is a difficult apprenticeship, but it has to be tried. For instance, if we are in joy and in love with writing, we should try to write the *imund book*. The imund book deals with things, birds, and words that are forbidden by Those He.

The imund book is the book without an author. It is the book written with us aboard, though not with us at the steering wheel. It is the book that makes us experience a kind of dying, that drops the self, the speculating self, the speculating clever "I."

It's the book of the Act of Writing. The book that takes life and language by the roots. It has nothing to do with mad books—or with pornographic books. It's the book stronger than the author: the apocalyptic text, whose brilliance upsets the scribe. How can it be written? With the hand running. Following the writing hand like the painter draws: in flashes. The hand leads to the flowers. From the heart where passions rise to the finger tips that hear the body thinking: this is where the Book (*Alive*)-*to-Live* (*le livre Vivre*) springs from . . .

◧

I have a feeling it's time to finish this race. I have talked about *school*, not *goals* or *diplomas* but places of learning and maturing. Because even if there is, in the person writing, "an aptitude for fairyhood," a relationship to legend, a state of creation—this is not enough.

We must work. The earth of writing. To the point of becoming the earth. Humble work. Without reward. Except joy.

School is interminable.

I am trying to conclude. Suddenly, as it was page 158–and the third hour was ending, I realized that perhaps there must be "conclusions" to my journeys, because these sheets I'm walking across with my hand are "lectures." But there is no "conclusion" to be found in writing . . .

NOTES

The School of the Dead

1. Franz Kafka, *Wedding Preparations in the Country and Other Posthumous Prose Writings,* tr. C. Kaiser and G. Wilkins (New York: Schocken), p. 329.

2. *Ibid.*, p. 48.

3. Thomas Bernhard, "Trois journées," tr. Jean De Meur, in *Ténèbres—Textes, discours, entretien* (Paris: Editions Maurice Nadeau, 1986), pp. 57–58.

4. Marina Tsvetaeva, "My Pushkin," in *Marina Tsvetaeva—A Captive Spirit: Selected Prose,* ed. and tr. J. Marin King (London: Virago Press, 1983), p. 319.

5. Clarice Lispector, "Pertencer," in *A Descoberta do Mundo,* (Rio de Janeiro: Editora Nova Frontera, 1984), pp. 151–153.

6. Lydia Tchoukovskaia, *La Plongée,* tr. A. Bloch (Paris: Bibliothèque du Temps Présent, Editions Rombaldi, 1976).

7. Edgar Allan Poe, "The Facts in the Case of Mr. Valdemar," in *The Works of Edgar Allan Poe,* vol. 2 (London: Kegan Paul, Trench, 1884).

8. Primo Levi, *If This Is a Man—The Truce* (London: Abacus Sphere, 1986).

9. Fyodor Dostoyevsky, *The Notebooks for the Idiot,* tr. K. Strelsky (Chicago: University of Chicago Press, 1967), pp. 102–173.

10. Franz Kafka, *Letters to Friends, Family, and Editors,* tr. Richard and Clara Winston (New York: Schocken, 1978), p. 16.

11. Clarice Lispector, *The Hour of the Star,* tr. Giovanni Pontiero (Manchester: Carcanet, 1986).

12. Ingeborg Bachmann, *Der Fall Franza* (Munchen: Suhrkamp Verlag, 1983) pp. 7–8.

13. *Ibid.*

14. Paul Celan, "Schibboleth," in *Selected Poems,* translated by Michael Hamburger (New York: Persea, 1980), p. 82.

15. Thomas Bernhard, "Montaigne," *Die Zeit,* October 8, 1982, no. 41.

16. *Ibid.*

17. *Ibid.*

18. *Ibid.*

19. *Ibid.*

20. Edgar Allan Poe, "The Oval Portrait," in *The Works of Edgar Allan Poe*, vol. 2 (London: Kegan Paul, Trench: 1884), p. 545.

21. *Ibid.*, pp. 548–549.

22. Rainer Maria Rilke, *Das Testament* (Frankfurt: Insel Verlag, 1974).

23. Olga Borelli, *Clarice Lispector—Esboço para um possivel retrato* (Rio de Janeiro: Editora Nova Fronteira, 1981), pp. 49–50.

24. Franz Kafka, *Wedding Preparations in the Country*, p. 329.

25. Thomas Bernhard, *Ein Kind* (Salzburg und Wien: Resdenz Verlag, 1982).

26. Marina Tsvetaeva, "Pushkin and Pugachev," in *Marina Tsvetaeva—A Captive Spirit: Selected Prose*, p. 373.

27. Franz Kafka, *Wedding Preparations in the Country*, p. 99.

28. Ingeborg Bachmann, *Der Fall Franza*.

29. Jean Genet, "Le Funambule," in *Oeuvres complètes*, vol. 5 (Paris: Editions Gallimard, 1979), pp. 9–22.

30. Clarice Lispector, *The Passion According to G. H.*, tr. Ronald W. Sousa (Minneapolis: University of Minnesota, 1988), p. 3.

31. Clarice Lispector, *A Paixao segundo G. H.* (Rio de Janeiro: Editora Nova Fronteira, 1979), p. 5.

32. Clarice Lispector, *The Passion According to G. H.*, p. 3.

33. Clarice Lispector, "The Buffalo," in *Family Ties*, tr. Giovanni Pontiero (Austin: University of Texas Press, 1972), pp. 147–156.

34. Clarice Lispector, "The Crime of the Mathematics Professor," in *Family Ties*, pp. 139–146.

35. "The Story of the Black Id," in the French text "L'Histoire du ça noir." There is a play on words with *ça* (the Id), which slips close to *chat* (the cat) on a phonetic level.

36. Edgar Allan Poe, "The Black Cat," in *The Works of Edgar Allan Poe*, p. 421.

37. Marina Tsvetaeva, "My Pushkin," p. 372.

38. Franz Kafka, *Wedding Preparations in the Country*, pp. 429–30.

The School of Dreams

1. Sigmund Freud, *The Interpretation of Dreams*, tr. and ed. by James Strachey (New York: Avon, 1965); Ossip E. Mandelstam, *Mandelstam: The Complete Critical Prose and Letters*, tr. Jane Garry Harris and Constance Link (Ann Arbor: Ardis, 1979).

2. Clarice Lispector, *O Lustro* (Rio de Janeiro: Editora Nova Fronteira, 1982).

3. Franz Kafka, *Letters to Friends, Family, and Editors*, p. 16.

4. Ossip E. Mandelstam, "The Word and Culture," in *Mandelstam*, p. 112.

5. Franz Kafka, *Wedding Preparations in the Country and Other Posthumous Prose Writings*, tr. C. Kaiser and G. Wilkins (New York: Schocken), p. 253.

6. Franz Kafka, *Ibid.*, pp. 429–430.

7. Clarice Lispector, *O Lustro*, our translation, p. 57.

8. Clarice Lispector, "Love," in *Family Ties*, tr. Giovanni Pontiero (Austin: University of Texas Press, 1972), pp. 37–48.

9. *Ibid.*, pp. 39–40.

10. Clarice Lispector, "The Imitation of the Rose," in *Family Ties*, pp. 51–72.

11. Ossip Mandelstam, "Conversation About Dante," in *Mandelstam*, p. 7.

12. Hugo Von Hofmannstal, "The Wanderer," in *Selected Prose*, tr. Mary Hottinger and Tania and James Stern (New York: Pantheon, 1963).

13. *The Holy Bible*, Revised Standard Version (New York: Thomas Nelson and Sons, 1952), p. 21.

14. *Ibid.*

15. *Ibid.*, pp. 13–17.

16. Clarice Lispector, *O Lustro*, our translation, pp. 56–57.

17. *Ibid.*, our translation, p. 57.

18. *Ibid.*

19. *Ibid.*, p. 58.

20. Marina Tsvetaeva, *Art in the Light of Conscience*, tr. Angela Livingstone (Bristol: Bristol Press, 1991), pp. 68–69.

21. Since these dreams have been dreamt and written in French, the work of the signifier is lost in the translation. "*Reste le reste*": only the remains remain (Hélène Cixous's note).

22. Jean Genet, *Journal du voleur, Oeuvres complètes de Jean Genet* (Paris: Gallimard, 1949), p. 9.

23. Jean Genet, *The Thief's Journal*, tr. Bernard Frechtman (New York: Grove, 1964), p. 9.

24. Jean Genet, *Journal du voleur*, p. 9.

25. Jean Genet, *The Thief's Journal*, p. 9.

26. Arthur Rimbaud, "The Deserts of Love," in *The Illuminations*, tr. Louise Varèse (New York: New Directions, 1957), pp. 157–161.

27. Clarice Lispector, *O Lustro*, p. 7.

28. The convict prisons (*le bagne*) were penitentiaries where the convicts underwent their sentences of forced labor. These institutions no longer exist today.

29. Clarice Lispector, *The Stream of Life*, tr. Elizabeth Lowe and Earl Fitz (Minneapolis: University of Minnesota Press, 1989).

30. Clarice Lispector, *O Lustro*, p. 7.

31. *Ibid.*

32. *Ibid.*, p. 57.

33. *Ibid.*, pp. 57–59.

34. Marina Tsvetaeva, "Pushkin and Pugachev," in *Marina Tsvetaeva—A Captive Spirit: Selected Prose*, ed. and tr. J. Marin King (London: Virago Press, 1983).

35. *Ibid.*, p. 372.

36. *Ibid.*

37. Alexander Pushkin, *The Captain's Daughter,* tr. Nathalie Duddington (New York: Dutton, 1961), pp. 14–15.

38. Jean Genet, *Miracle of the Rose,* tr. Bernard Frechtman, (New York: Grove, 1966).

39. *Ibid.,* p. 282.

40. *Ibid.* pp. 282–286.

41. Clarice Lispector, *The Stream of Life,* p. 23.

42. Clarice Lispector, *The Apple in the Dark.* tr. Gregory Rabassa (Austin: University of Texas Press, 1986).

43. Thomas Bernhard, *Alte Meister—Komödie* (Frankfurt am Main: Suhrkamp Verlag, 1985).

44. Thomas Bernhard, *Ja* (Frankfurt am Main: Suhrkamp Verlag, 1978).

45. Jean Racine, "Athaliah," in *The Best Plays of Racine,* tr. Lacy Lockert (Princeton: Princeton University Press, 1957), pp. 341–343.

46. Clarice Lispector, "Love," in *Family Ties,* tr. Giovanni Pontiero (Austin: University of Texas Press, 1972).

47. Jean Genet, "What Remains of a Rembrandt Torn Into Four Equal Parts and Flushed Down the Toilet" (United States: Hanuman, 1988).

48. Clarice Lispector, *The Stream of Life,* p. 29.

49. Franz Kafka, *Wedding Preparations in the Country,* p. 231.

50. *Ibid.,* p. 248.

51. *Ibid.,* p. 141.

52. Arthur Rimbaud, "The Deserts of Love."

53. Ingeborg Bachmann, "Night Flight," in *In the Storm of the Roses: Selected Poems by Ingeborg Bachmann,* tr. Mark Anderson (Princeton: Princeton University Press, 1986), pp. 59–61.

54. Clarice Lispector, *The Stream of Life,* p. 23.

55. Franz Kafka, "The Wish To Be a Red Indian," in *The Penal Colony,* tr. Willa and Edwin Muir (New York, Schocken, 1948), p. 39.

The School of Roots

1. *The Holy Bible,* Revised Standard Version (New York: Thomas Nelson and Sons, 1952), p. 83.

2. *Ibid.,* pp. 22–24.

3. Clarice Lispector, *The Passion According to G. H.,* tr. Ronald W. Sousa (Minneapolis: University of Minnesota, 1988).

4. *Ibid.,* p. 64.

5. *Ibid.*

6. *Ibid.*

7. Hélène Cixous's italics.

8. Clarice Lispector, *A Paixao segundo G. H.* (Rio de Janeiro: Editora Nova Fronteira, 1979), p. 68.

9. Jean Genet, *The Thief's Journal,* tr. Bernard Frechtman (New York: Grove, 1964), p. 45.

10. Clarice Lispector, *The Passion According to G. H.,* p. 3.

11. *Ibid.*

12. *Ibid.*

13. *Ibid.*

14. Hélène Cixous's note: The translation reads: "I know," because the translation thinks that "I was knowing" sounds "unclean," incorrect. But let us keep the "incorrectness" of Clarice Lispector's text intact.

15. Clarice Lispector, *The Passion According to G. H.,* pp. 64–65.

16. *Ibid.,* p. 65.

17. Clarice Lispector, *The Stream of Life,* tr. Elizabeth Lowe and Earl Fitz (Minneapolis: University of Minnesota Press, 1989), p. 13.

18. Marina Tsvetaeva, "The Poem of the End," in *Marina Tsvetaeva: Selected Poems,* (Newcastle on Tyne: Bloodaxe, 1990), p. 136.

19. Hélène Cixous's italics.

20. Clarice Lispector, *The Stream of Life,* pp. 8–9.

21. Jean Genet, *The Thief's Journal,* p. 44.

22. *Ibid.*

23. *Ibid.*

24. *Ibid.*

25. Clarice Lispector, *The Stream of Life,* pp. 14–15.

26. Jean Genet, *The Thief's Journal,* p. 44.

27. *Ibid.,* pp. 44–45

28. *Ibid.*

29. *Ibid.*

30. *Ibid.*

31. *Ibid.*

32. *Ibid.*

33. *Ibid.*

34. *Ibid.,* pp. 44–45.

35. *Ibid.,* p. 45.

36. *Ibid.*

37. Translators' note, on *she-man* (*cette homme*): in the French text the feminine form of the demonstrative adjective *cette* is coupled with the masculine noun *homme* and thus plays on the borderline between the masculine and feminine forms.

38. Clarice Lispector, *The Stream of Life,* p. 13.

39. Jean Genet, *The Thief's Journal,* pp. 9–10.

40. Clarice Lispector, *The Stream of Life,* p. 44.

41. Franz Kafka, "Josephine the Singer; or, the Mouse Folk," in *The Penal Colony,* tr. Willa and Edwin Muir (New York: Schocken, 1948), pp. 256–277.

42. Jean de La Fontaine, *The Complete Fables,* tr. Norman B. Spector (Evanston: Northwestern University Press, 1988).

43. Franz Kafka, "A Dog's Searching," in *Kafka: Shorter Works,* tr. M. Pasley (London: Oxford University Press, 1973), pp. 148–184.

44. Clarice Lispector, *The Stream of Life,* pp. 45–46.

45. Franz Kafka, "Prometheus," in *Paraboles and Paradoxes* (New York: Schocken, 1961), p. 83.

46. Jean Genet, *Journal du voleur, Oeuvres complètes de Jean Genet* (Paris: Gallimard, 1949), pp. 52–53

47. Our change in the American translation is indicated in parenthesis.

48. Jean Genet, *The Thief's Journal,* pp. 47–49.

49. Hélène Cixous's italics.

50. Marcel Proust, *Remembrances of Things Past,* tr. C. K. Scott Moncrieff (London: Chatto and Windus, 1966), p. 1.

51. Hélène Cixous's change in translation is indicated in parenthesis.

52. Franz Kafka, *Wedding Preparations in the Country and Other Posthumous Prose Writings,* tr. C. Kaiser and G. Wilkins (New York: Schocken); *Diaries 1919–1923,* tr. Martin Greenberg (London: Mandarin, 1992).

53. Franz Kafka, *Wedding Preparations in the Country,* p. 51.

54. Jean Genet, *Journal du voleur,* pp. 27–28.

55. Jean Genet, *The Thief's Journal,* pp. 25–26.

56. Jean Genet, *Journal du voleur,* pp. 28–29.

57. Jean Genet, *The Thief's Journal,* p. 26.

58. Jean Genet, *Journal du voleur,* p. 30.

59. Jean Genet, *The Thief's Journal,* pp. 27–28.

60. Clarice Lispector, *The Stream of Life,* p. 17.

61. Franz Kafka, "Conversation Slips," in *Letters to Friends, Family, and Editors,* tr. Richard and Clare Winston (New York: Schocken, 1978).

62. *Ibid.*, p. 417.

63. *Ibid.*

64. *Ibid.*, p. 420.

65. *Ibid.*

66. *Ibid.*, pp. 419–421.

67. *Ibid.*, p. 422.

68. *Ibid.*, p. 423.

69. Olga Borelli, *Clarice Lispector—Esboço para um possivel retrato* (Rio de Janeiro: Editora Nova Fronteira, 1981), p. 61.

70. *Ibid.*